MOM STILL LIKES YOU BEST

Also by Jane Isay

WALKING ON EGGSHELLS

MOM STILL LIKES YOU BEST

The Unfinished Business Between Siblings

JANE ISAY

DOUBLEDAY

New York   London   Toronto   Sydney   Auckland

DOUBLEDAY

Copyright © 2010 by Jane Isay

www.doubleday.com

DOUBLEDAY and the DD colophon are registered trademarks of Random House, Inc.

Book design by Joseph Kaplan

Library of Congress Cataloging-in-Publication Data
Isay, Jane.
 Mom still likes you best : the unfinished business between siblings / by Jane Isay.—1st ed.
   p. cm.
 1. Brothers and sisters—Psychological aspects.
2. Brothers and sisters—Family relationships. I. Title.
 BF723.S43I83 2010
 306.875—dc22

                        2009027165

ISBN 978-0-385-52455-1

PRINTED IN THE UNITED STATES OF AMERICA

10 9 8 7 6 5 4 3 2 1

First Edition

For Jonathan

If you don't hate each other when you're young

How are you going to love each other when you're grown?

—A Brooklyn mother's mantra

CONTENTS

Part I
BEGINNINGS

1 JUST SO STORIES   3

2 THE CIRCUS TENT   22

3 WHY CAN'T YOU JUST GET ALONG?   38

4 LOOKING FOR LOVE IN ALL THE RIGHT PLACES   53

Part II
LIFE'S COURSE

5 GRAVITY SHIFTS   73

6 WHEN DIFFERENCE LEADS TO DISTANCE   91

7 THICK AND THIN   107

Part III
MAKING CHOICES

8 TRADING PLACES   129

9 MESSAGE IN A BOTTLE   145

10 BUILDING TOGETHER   161

ACKNOWLEDGMENTS   177

MOM STILL LIKES YOU BEST

Part 1

BEGINNINGS

1

JUST SO STORIES

I watch my three-and-a-half-year-old grandson dealing with his baby sister. He tells me he loves her and misses her when he stays over at my house. I think it's cute, but my son says it's a lie. One weekend, the whole family came with me to the shore, and every time Benji noticed one of the adults doing more than just feeding or changing the baby, he would make a beeline for her. "Ruby, I love you," he'd say, rushing to plant a kiss on her head. These airborne attacks of love scared me, because they were a little too energetic. He wanted to hold her hand or pat her all the time, especially when she was on my lap. Benji is an articulate and affectionate little boy, and I could see him working overtime to act like a big boy when he was around the baby. He loves his little sister, but he does not understand—and cannot really control—the strong feelings she evokes in him. The baby uttered her first laugh at Benji's antics, and she never lets him out of her sight. She's already attached to him. He will be her idol and model, and he will be good to her, I know. But his struggle to get used to the baby, his effort to deal with the unfairness he feels when her needs come first, his attempts both to control his anger and to understand the limits of his love reminded me of what we all experienced as kids. Watching them a year later, I see how his efforts to be a good older brother have created a bond of deep affection.

Recently I eavesdropped on a young family sitting next to me in a restaurant. The little boy had plunked himself down in the seat that was needed for his little sister's high chair. The father asked him to move to the banquette, to make room for the baby. The little boy was adamant. He refused to change seats. Folding his arms across his chest, this five-year-old wore a look of pure rage. He didn't cry or scream, but the anger and determination turned his little mouth into a dark circle. He eventually relocated to the other side of the table, but his mood did not change until a kind waitress distracted him and he joined the family meal. Later, as they were leaving the restaurant, I saw the boy take his father's hand and say, "I guess I'll have to marry her." "No," his father replied, "you won't." "Why not?" "It's against the rules." This little boy was in the process of learning the rules.

That brunch, with all its conflicting emotions, represents one of countless moments in the lives of kids as they learn to live with the fact that they must make room for others. First children have no reason to doubt their centrality—until the new baby arrives. Second children—the interlopers—rarely get the sole attention of the parents, and they often are greeted with jealousy and hostility by the former titleholder. Subsequent siblings are born into more complicated social situations, and they soon learn to navigate a complex world of loyalties, coalitions, and betrayals.

As adults, we may remember bits and pieces of those early experiences, but we generally have forgotten the intensity of our feelings. That intensity is the hallmark of childhood, and watching our own kids or our grandchildren reminds us of the amazingly strong bonds forged in the nursery. When young siblings are unsupervised, the time they spend together gives them the opportunity to experience every imaginable emotion and to express their feelings unfettered by the adults in their lives. Might makes right, older kids hold the power, younger ones snitch and bite; they steal from each other, tease each other, make each other cry, grab each other's toys, pinch each other's arms, and sneak each other's food. In (almost) the words of the *Monk* theme song, "It's a jungle in there." By the same token, children give each other a degree of support and comfort they cannot find elsewhere. A child with a nightmare crawls into his brother's bed; a sister hugs her brother who has been wronged; little soldiers venture into the adult world to protect their siblings. A beloved blanket is found; a doll is mended; a tear is wiped away. Loyalty and loving acts also form the bedrock of nursery behavior.

Children are either/or people. They go from "I love you!" to "I hate you!" in an instant. Brothers and sisters evoke powerful feelings a hundred times a day, and they often switch tracks, finding each other alternately a burden and a gift. Having a sibling is both. We were scared by our siblings' actions, and sometimes we shocked ourselves by the force of our anger. We loved them with a power that is hard to recover, and sometimes we wanted to kill them. Learning how to balance positive and negative feelings is a major task of childhood, as is the ability to deal with our siblings' hurt feelings, rages, and cruelties—as well as our own. These early moments when we expressed love and hatred, laughter and loyalty all happened before we had a full understanding of the world, before our brains developed the ability to reason or use logic. This explains both the profundity of the connection and the selective amnesia that many people over thirty have about their childhood experiences. Many of these events happened too early for us to remember and were felt too powerfully for us to fully forget.

From the hundreds of stories I've heard over the last years, I've found that nursery behavior exhibits at least five of the Seven Deadly Sins: Gluttony (they stuff their own faces to keep others from getting the goodies), Greed (they want everything the others have, and will steal to get it), Wrath (oh, the explosions), Envy (including secret pleasure at a sibling's disappointments), and Pride (the joy of outdoing a brother or sister). These sins may be deadly to the church, but at home they aren't. We understand this behavior as ordinary and expectable childhood responses to conflict and competition. Parents have a responsibility to keep their children from harming one another. But their authority over feelings is limited. It is the brothers and sisters who teach one another the lifelong lessons of getting along—or not. Home is the first schoolroom for the education of the emotions. It is a relatively safe place in which to express and experience raw emotions—after all, it's home. This is the gift.

By the same token, five of the Seven Virtues emerge in these early years: when a small child shows her grandmother how she helps her little sister fall asleep, Love is present; a child's sense of Justice is honed when he and his brothers begin to recognize what is fair, even when they are fighting; Courage can be seen in the playground when a small boy defends his older sister from the class bully; Restraint arrives when a girl stops herself in the middle of pulling her sister's hair and wonders what she could have been thinking; Hope can be seen in the eyes of a sister, standing on the sidelines of the hockey field, cheering on her special needs brother.

We are all capable of this mix of vices and virtues, and we experiment on our siblings. Some nursery behavior on a play date would probably mean permanent social exile, but the farthest place to which a brother or sister can be exiled is the bedroom or what some families call the "naughty chair." It is no wonder that adults remain powerfully connected to—or distanced from—their siblings, even after the years have softened their memories.

When we are grown, old childhood feelings can sneak up on us and overtake us, and when we are together time has a funny way of telescoping. Memory flashes beyond our control emerge from a long-ago time when we were trying to make sense of our world with the limited understanding of children. They are pure emotion, unfettered by reason. Even when we're in our seventh and eighth decades, brothers and sisters can still push our buttons. This is the burden.

Things can be going smoothly when, all of a sudden, something slams us back to childhood. "She was always judgmental," a woman will think of her elder sister after they have clashed about where to go for lunch. The tone more than the words raises the old antagonisms, powerful feelings that are thoroughly out of proportion to the dispute. Or a small detail can beam us back to the tender times of our childhood. Visiting my brother after many years, I caught sight of a tiny child's cardboard suitcase sitting atop a tall cabinet. My brother had carried it all through Europe when he was a small boy traveling with my mother, in the late 1930s. They pasted stickers of each country they visited on the suitcase, along with the icon for the

Cunard Line. This battered relic of his childhood—I was born after they came home—brought me a rush of deep sympathy for this little boy, who is now over seventy.

I'm not suggesting that any of us regress to our childish states of being; that would be a disaster. But I have learned that in the process of growing up and dealing with those passions, we may misunderstand our brothers and sisters. We see them through the eyes of an adult, but we are experiencing them with the primitive feelings of a child. The inability to revise our childish responses keeps us in a bind. Some people may be able to reconnect with distant siblings by seeing their memories through grown-up eyes and reframing their past. But first, people may need to reconnect with their childhood experiences.

Men and women in their twenties have greater access to these feelings because they are still in the thick of it. People in this age group, which I think of as the Gmail Generation, are in continuous touch with everybody, enjoying the smorgasbord of communications from Facebook, to Gchat, to Twitter. Unlike many of their elders, they are still passionately engaged with brothers and sisters. Some of them value their siblings as islands of permanence in a sea of change. "I see my sisters as one of the few constants in my life," one twenty-something woman told me. "You meet a lot of people you're not going to know for long, and so we increasingly turn to our siblings." Others are enjoying their new distance from the siblings with whom they fought as children. One woman mentioned that her sister was spending the summer in her town. "Is she moving in with you?" I asked. She shook her head. "I could never live with her again."

Brothers and sisters in their twenties are still resolving the old conflicts, and they hurt each other's feelings, endure miscommunications, fight, make up, and start all over again. They offer a window onto the intensity of childhood interactions, and we can observe their efforts to calm down and grow up. Stepping away from the hearth and into the world, these young people struggle to resolve their childish competition and dependence, anger and guilt. They offer a vivid portrait of siblings, in love and war.

Competition is the mother of all sibling relations, as we know from the books and the research. It can separate brothers and sisters, and it can also generate growth and change. Stephanie is still in the grips of lifelong rivalry—but it is beginning to ease just a bit.

READY, SET, GO

It's a cold February day, and Stephanie, a tall and slender woman of twenty-three, settles herself on the couch in my study and pulls a photograph out of her purse. It is a picture of her and her sister, who is two years older. They look like twins, with their dark hair and enormous almond eyes. She offers a commentary: "I was a little bit skinnier than her always, a little taller, and tanner—and had better skin than her." Stephanie is proud of acing out her sister on looks, and I begin to understand that the picture she holds is one of her scorecards. The sisters do not get along. They have been pushing each other's buttons forever. Her older sister was smart enough to employ the tool small children often use when the baby is born and they aren't happy: temper tantrums. What else can a two-year-old do but scream and stamp?

Stephanie likes to talk things through and chew on problems, but her short-tempered sister is a type A personality who knows what she thinks and doesn't have time for discussion. This older sister, like many first children, is the better student. Stephanie, like many younger children, is the one who always had friends. She is still close to her best friend from elementary school, and they created a gaggle of six girls who did everything together. Stephanie's sister resented being left out, was jealous of Stephanie's circle, and she felt awful when Stephanie chose to be with friends instead of with her. Stephanie tells two stories that characterize their relationship.

In the first story, Stephanie is the perpetrator. She and her best friend did everything together. Her sister was crushed when Stephanie went with her best friend, not her sister, to get their first tattoo. This rite of passage for young teenagers is a moment of shared pain and intimacy. It was a slap in the face.

The second story tells of her sister's temper. "I broke my own necklace, by accident. She was convinced that I broke it on purpose because she wore it sometimes—and she thought that I broke it to hurt her." So far this sounds like an ordinary accessory brawl, but things got out of hand: "We were screaming at each other and then she took a knife and started chasing me around the kitchen." With the help of the babysitter, Stephanie found sanctuary behind the locked door of her bedroom.

Everybody has Just So Stories of their childhood. These dramatic stories serve an important purpose. They help us explain to ourselves how we came to feel the way we do about our brothers and sisters and to justify our behavior. Embellished over the years, in the acts of remembering, telling and retelling, these stories are the emotional cornerstones of our sibling relationships. By the time we reach adulthood, they may not be entirely accurate, but they matter because they have a kernel of emotional truth. Stephanie is not only telling me about getting a tattoo and a chase with a knife; she is telling me how much her winning the competition for friends hurt her sister, and about how scary her sister's temper was.

The sibling wars eased when Stephanie's sister went away to college and Stephanie began to miss her just a bit. But when they both were home from college, Stephanie hurt her sister's feelings when she ran out to be with her friends.

After leaving college and entering the real world, these sisters are gradually becoming allies instead of rivals. Stephanie lost her Wall Street job in the recession. She was miserable, and she turned to her older sister, who was a help. "You are doing great. I would be on the floor, bawling and crying," she would say when Stephanie called in despair. "I'm so impressed with you—I can't believe how you're pulling yourself together." Stephanie began to prefer her sister's counsel to that of her friends. "She's gone through a couple of full-time jobs and she knows what that's like."

Stephanie is beginning to respect some of her sister's choices—including the decision to focus on schoolwork instead of partying with friends—because she thinks her sister, who is enrolled in a prestigious MBA program, has a more reliable future. Now she is rethinking her choices. Why didn't she work harder in school, she wonders. Maybe her life wouldn't be so tempestuous now. Admiration for her sister's hard work mixes with jealousy, and Stephanie's eyes fill with tears even as she praises her sister.

So the distance and tension persist. When Stephanie had a momentary thought that it might be nice for them to share a beach house for a week this summer, the idea came and went in a nanosecond: "Well, she's someone who I need to have in small doses." The competition between these two sisters may die down over time, as their careers and lives progress. But you can hear, in Stephanie's stories and tone, the jealousy and unhappiness that came between them.

Adam and his little brother don't suffer from as much competition. And even though his brother has tried like the devil to be just like Adam, it never worked. These brothers had the great advantage of looking different, acting different, and having different personalities. Adam is quiet and studious; his younger brother is loud and gregarious. Adam is like their mom, and closer to her; his brother is like their dad, and closer to him. They have distinctly different styles. Here's an example: "My father and he are huge shoppers," says Adam, "where my mother and I are much more frugal. So they'll go into a store for milk and come out with a television. My mother and I get very frustrated."

Imagine these brothers boxing in a ring, and then each going to his corner at the end of the round. Adam's quiet mother comforts him, while their boisterous father calms his brother down. They consciously chose not to compete directly, and they were lucky to have such different temperaments and interests. Only on the ski slopes did the family allow competition, and this pair of brothers wrote the story of their lives in the snow.

TRACKS

They fought like two puppies, wrestling, biting, and punching. These boys, born three years apart, were always at each other's throats. Here's Adam's iconic story: "We were sitting on the stairs and he was teething, and he had these two little beaver teeth—and he sunk them into my shoulder. I grabbed his arm and yanked it, and pulled it out of the socket." Adam wasn't blamed, everybody cried, and the doctor reset the baby's shoulder.

The baby grew into a strong-minded and assertive guy, larger than Adam in every way. "He's like an R-rated version of me," Adam says. "All the things that I won't say, he'll say louder." He also outweighs Adam by twenty pounds. This little brother was infuriating when they were growing up. He was especially annoying around Adam's friends, whom he would never let alone. "He always had something to prove to them. He would wrestle with them and fight with them," Adam tells me. His brother was always louder and more assertive than Adam. When he describes his brother during these years, Adam doesn't mince words: "He was a scrappy little shit." Adam's second iconic story takes place at the telephone. His brother's friends would call and say, "Is Adam there?" And he would literally say, "Fuck you, fag" and hang up the phone.

Still, even when they fought (and they did) or hurt each other (which they did), these brothers always made up. Adam sums up those years: "I didn't love him any less. I just wanted to kill him." The little brother's louder and more assertive personality left Adam plenty of room to grow into the promising young scholar he is today, and Adam's focus on his studies gave his little brother plenty of room to be the successful salesman he is today.

The only area in which they were active rivals was on the ski slopes. The family lived in Vermont and spent all their free time together on skis. Adam, the older, was always the stronger skier. He loved it so much that he took a year off after high school to be a ski bum in the Rockies. After they both graduated from college, the brothers took a trip to South America, where they skied their hearts out. Adam used his little video camera to document their vacation—and their ski competition. He still beat his little brother, although not by a wide margin. The final cut of that video, Adam tells me, is one of his brother's favorite things. It documents not only their competition but also the good times they shared.

Now Adam is teaching in the Midwest, and his brother has moved out to the Rockies, where he works in sales during the week and spends his weekends on the slopes. Just this year, the family took a ski vacation to celebrate their father's sixtieth birthday. They did some magnificent slopes, and it was the perfect birthday week for their dad. Something else important happened. His brother had become the stronger skier, and Adam acknowledged it. Those years of winning on the slopes were over for him.

But because they have such different lives now, and because they have always loved each other, Adam ceded the top spot not only with grace but with pride. He is watching his little brother mature in other areas, including his relations with Adam's friends. "He makes a positive impression on people," Adam says. "I'm very proud to see him grow into that. I think that's one of the joys of an older sibling: seeing their younger sibling grow into a man or a woman that they become proud of." You can't take pride in the accomplishments of a younger brother or sister, I think to myself, unless you have had a role in that success. The bond is stronger because of it.

Accentuating differences is a natural response to direct competition. People are born with a great enough range of traits and grow up with a variety of opportunities, so it is relatively easy to choose different paths. Serena and Venus Williams are a counterexample, but they have harnessed their competition so that when they aren't beating each other, they are beating everybody else. The urge to be different is one of the benefits of sibling rivalry. Young people are forced to dig deep into themselves and find out who they are—not who their parents want them to be, not who their siblings are.

A friend of mine in her twenties who is close to her older sister remarked, "We are such different people. We have essentially the same personality and way of looking at the world, but our talents are different." This differentiation has been a great boon. "Our interests diverged enough when we got to high school that we really were in a harmonious place with sibling rivalry. My sister is a type A personality. Super organized, super good with money. I am impulsive and creative, into writing and the arts. I would help edit her essays, and she would help me through math problems."

We cannot know how much of this variance is genetic and how much is environmental. But we do know that the law of small changes means that when we focus on tiny variations and develop them with energy, they can turn into large differences. I think that's why so many brothers and sisters develop along different lines.

Scrappy kids (my friend used to lick her older sister's arm when she was pinned down on the floor), they are good sisters in their twenties. Of course, their relationship is not without its quirks. The older sister is a health nut, and she nags my friend about her soft-drink habit. In return she gets digs about her type A personality. This might give the appearance of conflict, but as my friend says, "I imagine we'll have *Odd Couple*–style sisterly tiffs for many years to come."

People who do not get along would give the world for a relationship that included *Odd Couple* sisterly tiffs. When Laura was young, she thought that she and her sister would always be enemies. But they had the very good fortune of changing places.

"SHE BEAT ME INTO THE WOMAN I AM"

Take a strong-minded little girl of four who has been the center of attention all her (short) life, and who has ruled her indulgent parents with her volcanic temper, and tell her that her mother is having a baby. She accepts the reality, but requires that her mother bring home an older brother.

Furious when a tiny baby sister arrives, this adorable and charming girl takes every opportunity to bop the baby over the head. "My sister was in such a state that our parents bought her a dog," the former baby, now a successful executive in her late thirties, says, "because they thought it would distract her from trying to kill me." Terrified, Laura would scream her head off whenever her sister came into the room. The antagonism and physical torture persisted into adolescence. Mental torture in the form of belittling and criticism, rage and intimidation were Laura's daily fare. She returned the favor by being a thoroughly annoying brat, messing with the older girl's things, intruding on her when she was with her friends, and humiliating her in front of the boyfriends.

Like all younger children, Laura idolized her older sister.

This girl may have been mean, but to Laura she was perfection, everything Laura wanted to be and wasn't. The two sisters didn't look alike. Laura is a striking woman with cascades of reddish hair surrounding her heart-shaped face. Her older sister is petite and dark. So tiny, swarthy women are Laura's ideal of beauty. And Laura knew, as all younger siblings do, that she could never catch up to her sister. Her sister was four years older, and she would always be way ahead. These sisters epitomized Margaret Mead's famous teaching to her students, "Beware the sibling wars."

Where were the parents during these years? They were of the "stay out of it" persuasion, a common and sane point of view when dealing with siblings at war in the nursery. Laura understands and respects that, but she feels that she and her sister could have used a little help in resolving their differences. The sisters slipped into a steady state of intimidation, on the one hand, and distancing, on the other. Laura was relieved when her sister left for college.

But when their father died, the girls had no choice but to collaborate in dealing with their bereft and helpless mother. Still, her sister was a carper and critic, and Laura would go quiet, or leave the room, or get off the phone when things got rough. Laura was better than her sister at self-control—she knew that silence protects you from anger. Nevertheless, she believed she was an inferior being, and she continued to put up with unacceptable levels of meanness because she didn't know anything different. Resigned to this difficult relationship, she leaned toward distance over conflict, a choice many people prefer.

Laura recalls the moment when things began to change. She was in her college dorm room with her friends when her sister dropped by. Laura was trying on a dress that she planned to wear to a dance that weekend. "One of my good friends was there," Laura says, "and a couple of other girls from the dorm. My sister said something insulting and discouraging about how I looked in the dress. My friend turned to her and said, 'We all like Laura, and she looks beautiful in that dress, and if you're going to be like that, you need to leave.' " That was a revelation. A college friend had validated Laura's perception that her sister was mean, and had taken her to task for it. Laura thought, "She really is mean to me, and I can do something about it." This moment marked the beginning of a shift in the power structure between the sisters. Her friend's comment had shut her sister up; maybe Laura could do the same. The next time her sister got on her back for no reason, Laura told her to stop.

Responding like an adult, not a cowering child, Laura began to shift her sister's attitude a bit. Over time, Laura realized two things: First, that on occasion she might be right in thinking that her sister was genuinely out of order (something her parents never admitted). Second, it dawned on her that she could tell her sister off and survive. It's not as if her sister suddenly grew a new personality; to this day she is temperamental. But Laura began to show her that these outbursts could have consequences. Because she had to deal with an adult and couldn't push her around so easily, her sister began to sense that Laura might be more than the bratty little intruder she'd hated when she was four.

A further insight came when Laura realized that her sister was not perfect. This happened when they shared an apartment. Laura didn't know if they could survive under the same roof, but it kind of worked. Laura suspected that her sister's choice of husband was not so great, and that she wasn't as divinely happy as she wanted everyone to believe. He was always critical of Laura and her mother, but she began to see that maybe he wasn't nice to her sister, either. When the marriage fell apart, Laura made an important call to their mother. "My mom could say really hurtful things and be very judgmental, and so I called to tell her to just be supportive." It may have been a relief for her sister to know that her former victim had become an ally who would intercede on her behalf. Their roles began to change as the little one became protective of the older one.

Gradually, a new pattern of collaboration overcame the carping, which was a good thing because a few years later their mother became ill, and the sisters needed each other. The last months of their mother's life were torture for all three women: emergency trips to the hospital; flights from both coasts to Chicago; a nursing mother trying to keep it together in the ICU (by this time the sister had remarried and had a little baby); a freshman employee risking her new job to leave town and care for her mom. When their mom died, the sisters were exhausted, bereaved, but totally bonded. They disposed of their mother's possessions without a ripple and then took a long weekend in the Indiana Sand Hills to recuperate.

Fifteen years later, the sisters speak on the phone four or five times a day. When one takes a vacation outside the country, the other is uneasy. They chatter to each other from department store to office ("I found these shoes, they almost match my blue dress, but they're not open-toed. What do you think?" "Take them home and see if they work. You can always return them") and from car to schoolyard ("What about that bully who's been after Toby?" or "Henry's sister is in a royal mess," or "What are you making for dinner?"). How did this happen? In stages. I call it a pas de deux. Laura prefers to think of it as clogging.

Here are the steps these sisters took:

- Laura recognized that she wasn't crazy to think her sister was being mean to her and slowly began to correct her notion of herself as an inferior creature.
- Setting limits on her sister's cruelty served notice that Laura was no longer a helpless little girl.
- The sisters lived under the same roof for three months without committing murder, which affirmed the possibility of an enduring relationship.
- Laura protected her older sister in a moment of crisis.
- They collaborated in the care of their dying mom.

Over these hard and sad years, the sisters shed their childhood roles. Of course, with their parents gone, they cling to each other, but there are plenty of siblings who cannot walk this path together. The tragedy of losing both parents when they were young hovers over their story, and the strength of their bond is certainly related to it. The connection between love and death haunts Laura.

"I don't know whether this is something that other people do, but I kill people. I imagine how my life would be without them. When I try it with my sister, I stop. I just can't imagine it, I can't bear it, and I can't imagine her children without her. I can't imagine any of that without her. It would be the most devastating thing in my life if I lost my sister."

Credit Laura with bringing her sister to the level of maturity that made their closeness possible. The quiet one, the one who was always torn down, became the leader. The dance of these two sisters became a loving duet.

We tell ourselves Just So Stories about our brothers and sisters in order to make sense of our relationships in the present. How we feel about our brothers and sisters today has everything to do with the stories from childhood we tell ourselves as adults. We can make them frightening or amusing—it all depends on how we have decided to live with (or without) our brothers and sisters. Stephanie still feels guilty about how she hurt her sister's feelings, and she is still intimidated by her sister's personality, so her stories convey anxiety. Adam's stories of his brother's capacity to be infuriating are infused with humor and ease. Sure, he was a royal pain, but he's grown up a lot, and they love each other. Laura's stories of her childhood and adolescence are both operatic and triumphant, because she and her sister traveled a great distance to find each other.

As adults we have the opportunity to choose how we deal with our Just So Stories. It is entirely possible to change tone, as we get older. One of the tools that help us turn the dark memories into lighter ones is knowledge of the context. As kids, we didn't have sufficient information about what was happening behind closed doors, or in the world beyond our homes. And as kids our brains had not developed the analytic capacity to understand the true dynamics of our families. Children think that they and their siblings are the stars of the play. It turns out that they are not the major actors. The next chapter shows how factors beyond their control influenced relationships between brothers and sisters.

2

THE CIRCUS TENT

I remember the first time I went to the circus. It was an amazing blend of color, sound, and smell. When I felt overwhelmed by the noise and activity, I would look up at the many slender poles holding up this huge structure. The lightness of the poles and the enormousness of the tent seemed a miracle to me. How could that be? What I didn't know about, and couldn't see, was the hidden system of ropes, pulleys, and weights that kept the great swaths of cloth in place and held the circus tent aloft. That's a good way to think of our childish understanding of what was happening with our brothers and sisters. At the circus we saw the animals, we heard the music, and the experience was unforgettable. But we had no idea what was going on behind the scenes. As children, we were ignorant of the family structures that were passed down through the generations, the pushes and pulls between our parents, and the forces that were beyond a child's control. In a way, we all grew up in the circus tent of our family. Our brothers and sisters may have been the clowns or the lions or the aerialists: funny, frightening, or amazing. But we had no idea about the structure that shaped our experiences.

It makes perfect sense that what we experienced as children has more complex and subtle causes than we possibly could have known. Childish explanations are not useful, because they are based on incomplete information and immature reasoning. So children who are not favored blame the one who is; children feel abandoned by siblings who leave home at a young age for their own reasons; kids whose genetic makeup is more like one parent's than another's don't understand how the affinity—or irritation—came about. After kids blame the offending sibling, they tend to blame themselves. It is not uncommon for these childish explanations—laced with resentment or guilt—to frame a relationship for life.

Understanding a broader context—of elements beyond our control or the control of our siblings, of facts that we might not have known, of situations beyond our ability to change—can bring relief. And in families where the connections have remained strong and close, attention to the context can bring an extra smile—and a lesson or two. Sometimes people who don't have what they want from their siblings don't quite know where to turn. An understanding of the unseen elements that are beyond our ken or our control can help. Knowledge breeds empathy, which can help break up old hostilities and salve ancient hurts.

MY BROTHER WAS AN ONLY CHILD

Take Raymond, for example; he is now retired from decades of teaching English in a big-city high school. An admirable man, he has built a good life with his wife of over thirty years. They have lots of friends, travel as much as they can afford, and their kids are growing up well; that's all good news. But there is another side to Raymond's life, and it concerns his brother.

Raymond's is a story of loss and longing. His brother was seven years old when Raymond was born. "We were seven and a half years distant," he tells me, emphasizing his choice of words, the way an English teacher would. Raymond used to joke that his brother was an only child; in fact, he was just that for the seven years before Raymond appeared. It seems that his brother welcomed Raymond and was very good to him. He taught Raymond to play cards and spent countless hours helping him with schoolwork. Raymond tells me that the card games encouraged his interest in math, which he almost majored in—until a professor guided him to his real talent, which was writing. You can see the love on Raymond's face as he speaks about his brother. He thought that their closeness would never end. But that did not happen.

Their home was not a pleasant place, and that may be why his brother was so protective. Raymond describes his mother as cold and manipulative, which he blames on her tragic family background, and he tells me his father was brutal. Coming home after a long day at work, his father would, at their mother's direction, slap the boys' faces for punishment. Then she would yell at him for making her boys cry. Raymond's brother warned him, "Don't fight with Mom and Dad. You can't win. Just *yes* them until you can get out." Raymond's brother took his own advice: he had jobs afternoons and weekends through high school, then went away to college and never came home again. He married a woman who didn't care for the family, either, and that was the end of their ties to Raymond's family. The wife didn't have anything against Raymond, but he made the decision to stay close to his parents, and soon the young married couple was lost to him. Raymond thought he could be more successful in dealing with his parents. He never did change them. (Who ever does?) "But," he says, "I kept fighting, and I think that kept me sane." That may have been just what Raymond needed to do, but by then his brother was gone.

This has been Raymond's sorrow all his life. He kept looking to replace his brother—at work, among friends. His yearning troubled him so much that he went into therapy, thinking that he might be homosexual because of his longing for this closeness with another man. Raymond tells me he isn't gay; he was overwhelmed by the longing to get his brother back.

Then his brother's wife died, and the men started to reconnect. They spoke regularly, and they shared the occasional evening of music or theater. Raymond wanted real conversation, not sitting side by side watching a performance in silence, not news bulletins or stories from his brother's day at work. Raymond never doubted that his brother loved him, but he wanted intimacy. Sadly, there was not enough time to reestablish the old bond, because soon after he lost his wife, his brother was diagnosed with lung cancer.

Raymond visited the hospital every day. Since his brother was on oxygen and had trouble speaking, Raymond did most of the talking. As he left at the end of each visit, Raymond would lean over the bed to plant a kiss on his brother's forehead, saying, "I love you." What he heard through the mask was "My brother, my brother." Six weeks later, his brother was gone. Those words are his powerful legacy, along with a substantial estate. Raymond is an aging hippie who doesn't care about money—he's trying to figure out how to give it away. What he yearned for and never found was his brother.

How many ways can you lose a brother, I think to myself. First, because his family was a difficult one and his brother departed to save himself; second, because Raymond decided to stay home and fight it out; third, when his brother's marriage completed the rift with the family; and fourth, when cancer took Raymond's brother. None of these things were Raymond's fault, and they weren't his brother's, either. Seven years is a big age gap between siblings. It is not uncommon for the first child to escape from a troubled family. Raymond refused to follow his brother out of the family. His ties to their parents and the age gap made it almost impossible for the brothers to stay connected. By now Raymond doesn't blame his brother or himself. But he is profoundly aware of what he didn't have, and what he has lost.

STORMY WEATHER

Connie, who is in her fifties, spent most of her life longing for a relationship with her older sister. But too many elements beyond the control of either girl conspired to keep them apart as kids and created a rift that seems unbridgeable in adulthood. They were born with different gifts and skills, but one girl met with their mother's ire and the other with acceptance.

Connie was twenty-one years old when her sister divorced her. It happened during her sister's wedding, at the reception following the ceremony. The bride sat Connie down at one of the empty tables. "She said she wanted me to know that I was a terrible person and she hated me, and that now that she was married and was going to have a family of her own, she would never have to speak to me again." They had never been close, these two sisters born a year apart. They were different from the start, and they received unequal treatment from their mother.

Genetics and family dynamics had set the stage for this divorce decades before.

Connie was an infant and her sister was a year old when their parents pulled up stakes in New England and headed to the desert, away from their large Irish Catholic family. They left for many reasons. This young couple felt overwhelmed by their families, which were close and robust, and intrusive. They wanted some distance. In addition, they believed that the hot, dry weather would relieve Connie's father's asthma. It turns out that the move may have been a large factor in the girls' distance from each other.

Their mother, a New Englander in a cowboy culture, a Catholic in a sea of Baptists, lacking any relief from her two babies and oppressed by heat in an era before home air conditioning, was overwhelmed and miserable. Connie remembers that her mom didn't have much energy for her daughters. At one point she went to the local priest and asked permission to go back to New England with the girls, since her husband needed to stay in the Southwest. The priest had a simple response. He said, "this marriage is going to make you miserable, and this is your route to heaven." Connie remembers their father as a loving and warm man who introduced his daughters to the outdoors and the natural world, as well as to the world of ideas. Had he lived, the girls might not have been so at odds, because his interests and style embraced them both, but the asthma took him too soon.

Their mother took her frustrations out on Connie's sister, who was gifted in ways that didn't fit the family or, to tell the truth, the times. She was athletic and mathematical, fascinated by how things worked. All these traits might have been fine in a little boy, but when Connie's sister took the clock apart to see how it ran or climbed the roof of their house, she came in for terrible punishment from her mother. Today a girl like that might be seen as a potential leader, but her sister was an outsider, a square peg in a round hole. Connie cannot remember a time when her mother wasn't screaming at her sister. You can guess the rest: Connie was a dreamy little girl who never got into trouble. While her sister was climbing the highest tree, Connie was sitting peacefully watching the leaves move against the sky.

Disparate temperaments and different treatment from their mother would have been enough to set the sister against Connie. She probably thought, as all first children do, that somehow Connie was the cause of her troubles. Then school happened. Connie's sister, with energy that today would probably be labeled ADHD, couldn't sit still. She was not beloved by the teachers, and this little girl who could add long columns of numbers in her head was almost dyslexic when it came to reading people. She didn't get their jokes, couldn't figure out what to wear, and felt very much a loner. You can fill in the blanks here, too. Connie, a reader, a placid child, was a natural with her peers. Connie quickly adjusted and fell into the classroom environment with ease. She soon became the leader when it came to social life, clothing, and parties. For some of their high school years, the sisters shared a circle of friends—the smart kids. But gradually Connie's sister drew away. Her love of the outdoors and animals was more compelling than the bright conversation, and soon she became critical of this group of kids. "She started saying these people were too shallow," Connie says, "and she didn't like being with them. And then she bought her first horse and really has been a ranch woman ever since."

As they grew up, other differences between them rankled. Connie's gradual falling away from the church was a big deal to their mother but was even more important to her sister. She hated the fact that Connie was not a faithful Catholic. I don't think that Connie gave it a second thought—she was headed to an Ivy League college and eager to participate in the heady world of the intelligentsia.

Connie has a hard time understanding what she did to deserve such strong dislike. What may have been simple jealousy in childhood turned into severe judgments as they grew up. Their lives have diverged even more: her deeply religious sister has a husband and two children; Connie never married, is childless, and long ago left the church. Connie's sister finds Connie selfish and useless; Connie cannot accept her sister's narrow view of the world.

Recently Connie had a weeklong visit from one of her grown nieces—an unusual event, since her sister wouldn't allow Connie to see the children when they were little. Toward the end of their time together, Connie's niece commented that she thought Connie was really nice. The comment took Connie aback. "Well," her niece said, "my mother always told us that you were a selfish person, and that the reason you never married was because you were too selfish to love children." This was crushing. "And here's the kicker," Connie says, "my sister told them that I hated children so much that I didn't want to be in the same house as her kids." The sad truth is that her sister wouldn't allow Connie any contact with them.

Connie tries to be philosophical. "For years I was either enraged or hurt, but at some point I made my peace and decided to give up. And then every once in a while, I'll feel bad. I don't see what I can do about it. But it's sad." Connie's voice gets low. "I mean, talking to you, I'm telling it as good stories, but it hurts my heart every time I think about it."

This story has one happy outcome. When she was in college,

Connie found a way to cope with the loss of her sister. She found a friend who has been her good sister for over thirty years. "We were passionate friends from nineteen on. She had a horrible mother, and I had a horrible sister. I think we have together what many sisters have." Good sisters, I think. "Can you fight?" I ask. "Yes, and then we make up." Connie continues, "I have many friends, but she is like blood. I remember once when her youngest son was eight or nine, it finally dawned on him that I wasn't a relative. That made me prouder than anything I'd ever heard."

Unlike Connie, Evelyn and her sisters weren't particularly looking for friends. They had each other, and they needed each other, because their family was always on the move. Her family was peripatetic, picking up stakes every time their father, a lifetime member of the military, was assigned to a new post. Their father's military bearing may have been a factor in the closeness his grown children still feel. It was a large family, with six kids born over two decades. Their father was a stern disciplinarian, and their mother was too distracted to choose favorites or engage in playground politics.

THE MORGANS PASS THE FROG AROUND

> *"We really care about each other, and value each other. They're all fascinating, wonderful, bright, smart people."*
> —Evelyn

Evelyn's father was a career army man. After his World War II stint in the Pacific, he landed a desk job in Australia, where he met and fell in love with an Australian secretary. The soldier and his war bride returned to the States with two daughters, Evelyn and her older sister. Four more children were born over the course of the next decades. Evelyn and her two sisters (another girl was born shortly after they got to the States) have always been close, but they loved the younger ones, too. Today the six of them are spread out all over the country, where they have careers in science and in the helping professions. They speak often; they are loving and proud of one another. Evelyn says they are all also proud to be in their family. Growing up was not so easy, and they always looked out for one another through those exacting times. Gratitude is part of this sibling mix.

Like all military families, they moved around the country, from base to base, about every eighteen months. Just as they were settling into a new school, adjusting to the new curriculum, making a team or finding good friends, they would have to pack up and move on. The itinerant life of these army brats was a factor in their closeness. The four oldest were "uprooted together, and replanted together," Evelyn says. She had the good luck to be the middle of the three oldest sisters. "I always felt privileged, because if my older sister wanted to do something, I was the natural person she'd ask to do it with. And if my younger sister needed a partner, it was me. So I was never left out." She says that some of them think she was the favorite of their parents, but she doesn't remember that. Her sisters were the people who mattered to Evelyn.

Their father was a military disciplinarian. Beds were checked for square corners, and not much affection was expressed. Their mother, who had her first child at twenty and her last child in her forties, wasn't fun and games, either. Evelyn tells me, "None of us kids ever wanted to be aligned with either parent. We loved them in our own ways, but we did not aspire to be like them."

When neither parent is easy, and when they don't pay the children much attention, the kids may bond together in behalf of one another. That's what happened in Evelyn's family: "If either of my sisters says, 'You remind me of Mom,' that's the last thing any of us wants to hear." This shared point of view created a strong sense of fellowship. The brothers and sisters wanted to fly the coop and make lives for themselves. Their father encouraged this. Each of his children was presented with a gift at their high school graduation: a suitcase. They took the hint. Evelyn credits some of their closeness to the fact that they live in different parts of the country. If they were all in the same town, she thinks, they might not have gotten along so well. In a way they have continued the peripatetic life of their childhood—they travel to see each other.

The three older girls were a unit when they were kids and still are, into their fifties and sixties. Every couple of years they get together for a weekend. They call it the Morgan Sisters' Reunion. "We'll take off and go somewhere for four or five days, just the three of us," Evelyn says. "And talk about everything from love to lipstick, what's going on, and who's in your life." One of the sisters gave this farewell speech: "I want you both to know that I'm here for you, no matter what, if you ever need me," which Evelyn says "expresses how we feel about each other."

After their mother died, they decided to hold an annual reunion on the anniversary of her death. The focus of the weekend is croquet, a game they have played since childhood. "There's a tournament with a prize, a frog that goes from person to person," Evelyn tells me. The winner brings the frog to the next reunion. A while ago, a couple of the brothers and sisters had taken their mother's ashes back to Australia, and at the next reunion they showed films of the little funeral they held there. "One night, we all took the cable car to the top of the mountain, had dinner there. Some breakfasts together, and hikes together, just hanging out." They part with tears: "It's as though you're never going to see each other again, even though you know you will." The physical distance between the six brothers and sisters, and the time that goes by between visits and even conversations might make you wonder how close they can really be. Here's one definition of closeness, offered by Evelyn about one of her sisters: "Sometimes, reading her e-mails, or letters, is like reading my own diary."

This group of siblings didn't get much coddling or attention. Planted and moved almost every year, they needed one another, and they had one another. The constant uprooting helped their fellowship, and so did their mother's self-absorption and their father's rigidity. They remain grateful for the support they gave one another as kids. Loving, accepting, gracious, happy when they meet, parting in tears, this can-do set of siblings can do for themselves and give one another just what they need. Their sense of self-reliance comes from the efforts they all exerted, and while they loved their parents, they knew they could count on each other.

Things have a different tone when the background noise for brothers and sisters is warmth and acceptance. They may find that closeness comes naturally. Some of them have the pleasure of knowing who is responsible for the joy they share. Millie and her brother and sister are clear about their mom, what she did for them, and what she means to them.

SWEET LAUGHTER

Three people are sitting in my study with me. It is a small room, and it is cramped, but we are having a ball. They are telling me about themselves and each other. Millie was the instigator of this joint interview. She brought her two siblings along with her so I could witness them interacting, because they have such a wonderful time together. At first, we were going to meet around their eighty-nine-year-old mother's table, but their mother decided that her kids would speak more freely without her. Her kids, Doris, Millie, and Jerry, are sixty-five, sixty-four, and fifty-six, respectively. The conversation is rollicking, funny, and full of interruptions. Nobody can finish a sentence, and nobody minds. When Jerry knocks over a glass of water, there is laughter—"Jerry, we can't take you anywhere"—and they tell me that they fight all the time but it never lasts. Years ago, Millie and her husband moved to Canada for several years, to be near Jerry and his family; they still spend great amounts of time together, and they speak to each other—and their mother—every day. Doris's quiet husband has an e-mail relationship with all his nieces and nephews, and the three siblings tell me they all helped raise each other's kids.

Doris and Millie were born a year apart and were treated and dressed as twins. Their grandmother, their mother's mother, lived with them until Millie was fourteen. The two women were very close and compatible, and their father loved his mother-in-law. Millie, the middle child, was the closest to Nonna, and her face still glows when she talks about her.

Jerry came along when Doris was nine and Millie was eight. They tell me that he was the most adorable baby. Doris leans over to pinch his cheek, but stops herself—I'm in the room.

The story goes that the neighbors were so excited about the arrival of a boy in the family that they lined the sidewalk outside their building to greet the baby as he was carried in from the car. Jerry was always loved and adored, and his smile shows it.

Their mother was a saleslady and didn't have time for things like Cub Scouts, so Millie sewed Jerry's badges and took him to den meetings. It didn't matter that their mom wasn't interested in such things. What really interested her were her three children. She never came home at the end of the day empty-handed. Maybe some days it was only a chocolate bar; on other days it would be something she thought one of them would like. She did not wait for birthdays. She didn't feel any compunction about bringing a gift for one of her children and leaving the others out, and they didn't get upset because they knew their turn would come. Their mom worked hard to even the playing field for them. So the clumsy daughter got dancing lessons and the daughter with hair too thick to braid had an adorable short haircut. These people were far from rich, but they grew up in an era where hardworking parents could provide a safe neighborhood, a good education, and a good life for their children. Doris tells me that she never felt the need for anything. The siblings nod in agreement.

This family laughs a lot. They laughed over Jerry's spilled glass of water and tell me of the time their parents were having trouble maneuvering a new sofa up the stairs. So when they got it to the landing, they just sat down on it and had a good laugh.

They tell me that it was very important to their mother that they love one another and be close, and they are. It seems natural to them that they should have so much fun with one another—their parents did. They adore "Mommy." She was a beauty as a young woman and has kept her looks. At the wedding of Doris's daughter, while the bridal party was lining up to go down the aisle, the caterer took their mother aside (she was eighty-five) and whispered, "You must have been something!" She always had a sense of style, and now the grandchildren consult her for fashion tips. She is smart about boundaries. When her married children lived on the ground floor of her house, she would come in the front door and head upstairs without bothering them. When her children moved to Canada, taking the grandkids with them, she never made a peep. Doris knew how sad she was, but didn't rat on her mother.

They say she has a strong ego, by which I think they mean she has confidence. She trusted her loving instincts, and they served her and her family well. Childhood friends who have moved away still visit with their "Mommy" when they come home—everybody just loves her, and with good reason, it seems.

Does this sound too good to be true? I spent hours with these people, and I watched them carefully. They adore one another, and the only thing that makes them sad is that some of their children do not have the same closeness. This trio has clearly forgotten the times when they weren't so close, when tensions arose and anger erupted. But the memories of their negative feelings—everyone has them—have been washed away in this sea of love and laughter. I suspect that these three never felt they were playing a zero-sum game, in which they had to compete for love and attention; there seems to have been plenty to go around.

After they left, I was sorry that their mother had not been in the room to hear her children express their love for one another—and for her. A couple of weeks later, Jerry e-mailed to ask if he could have a copy of the interview transcript. They wanted to present it to their mother as part of her ninetieth-birthday celebration. It was my pleasure.

Eventually the circus performance is finished and soon the animals are caged, the costumes are put away, and the entire tent is taken down and packed up. The circus heads to another town, but our own personal circus never leaves us. We may be thrilled by the beauty of the acrobats and frightened by the scary lions all our lives. Our childhood experiences and the conclusions we drew about ourselves and our siblings are very hard to let go of, because they were so intensely felt. I was telling my grandson last night about my first movie, *Snow White*. I got so scared by the poisoned apple that I cried and cried and had to be taken into the theater lobby to calm down. As I told him the story, my heart began to pound. That movie was as vivid last night as when I saw it many years ago. We hold the same kinds of memories from our childhood, those intense moments when our brothers and sisters played starring roles in our dramas. Understanding what was going on behind the scenes has great benefits for us: by seeing context, we may be able to salve our hurts, relieve our guilt, and celebrate the good times we had. Context allows us to replace our childhood images with more adult understanding and permits us to let our own memories grow up. It may offer us the chance to see our brothers and sisters as the people they are today, not the players in a long-ago circus.

3

WHY CAN'T YOU JUST GET ALONG?

A young man in his first job out of college lives at home, along with his older brother. "We're very close," he says. "But we get on each other's nerves a lot. I have a great time with him, but he can also drive me insane. And I can really get under his skin when the mood strikes me."

A woman in her fifties checks her caller ID when the phone rings. If she sees her little sister's name, she doesn't pick up. She worries about her sister all the time but can't deal with her demands.

"She was always such a downer," a woman in her seventies says about her sister. "I can't stand being with her." She visits with this sister regularly and always comes laden with gifts.

A seventy-five-year-old man I know has a fine relationship with his nearly eighty-year-old brother. He told me, "I love my brother, but it makes me crazy that he always drops his g's when we're talking."

People worry when they have reservations and complaints about their brothers and sisters; they feel terrible when they don't look forward to time together. Are they poor siblings? Are their relationships subpar? Is there something wrong with them? The answer to all these questions is no. I have found it common for people to harbor mixed feelings about their siblings. In addition to the wonderful moments together, they share a history of conflict, competition, and sometimes cruelty. That is an important part of what brothers and sisters do when they are young. They are learning the rules of competition, how to win and how to lose, how it feels to hurt the feelings of someone they love, and what it takes to help that person recover from hurtful behavior. Kindness and patience, assertiveness and temper—all these are tried out in the nursery, to good effect. We never lose the social skills we pick up at home with our brothers and sisters. Many of our habits of dealing with adult peers began there.

Having mixed feelings about brothers and sisters does not mean that you don't love them; it does not mean that you are somehow deficient. Fluctuating between feeling a deep connection and powerful irritation is common. People who are struggling with imperfect sibling relationships may feel better upon learning that they are far from alone. Perhaps they can stop blaming their siblings for being so annoying and stop blaming themselves for being overly sensitive—or vice versa. The ideal of brothers and sisters who are each other's best friends does exist, but it's not so common. It's an ideal, however, that parents often hold, even when they aren't speaking to their own siblings.

———

When children snipe and fight, parents ask an age-old question: Why can't you all get along? It's a good question, and an important one, but I think that instead of hearing, "Stop your fighting," many people hear, "You shouldn't have angry feelings toward your siblings and you should love them without reservation." We can't stop fighting, and we can't always be nice. We have to experience a wide range of our emotions before we can tame them. Those negative feelings sit right alongside the positive ones, and between the extremes are all the shades of gray: loving, liking, putting up with, being annoyed by, disliking—these are the realities of close relationships. The problem is that most people judge themselves as being less than good siblings when they veer away from the positive side of the range. That's ridiculous. Feeling all those shades of love and like and dislike is what it means to be close. It's the people who have come to believe that they have no feelings about their siblings who might be concerned. So long as there's a connection, there is the possibility of dialing from the negative to the positive. That's what we need to remember.

We can shine a kinder light on our relationships if we accept the universality of mixed feelings, if we understand that ambivalence is common, that our differences are the natural effect of growing up together, and that the ideal of perfect closeness and compatibility is just that—an ideal. There's a good answer to the question, How could we have come from the same womb? Becoming different from our siblings is part of the job of growing up. Conflict is inevitable, and we know better than anybody what makes them happy and what drives them up the wall. Fighting at home with brothers and sisters is part of the deal, no matter what the parents want. It takes extraordinary measures to make it stop. One woman told me that she and her two sisters were always at each other, forming teams of two against one all their lives. (She actually bit herself on the arm so as to draw blood and blamed it on her older sister.) When the girls were in high school, her distraught mother called them together and threatened: "I'll send each of you to a different Catholic high school if you don't stop this fighting." The girls loved their schools, so they declared a truce.

I think that we may be hardwired for ambivalence; our survival depends on it. We need to be able to see the glass as half full and half empty at the same time. People who think everything is rosy aren't realistic, and they don't look both ways when they cross the street. People who are thoroughly realistic get depressed and have difficulty facing the day.

The great British analyst D. W. Winnicott introduced the term the "good enough mother" to take the pressure off parents who were worried about failing to reach perfection. We might adapt that notion to siblings and be satisfied with being—or with having—a good enough brother or sister. Of course, some people do have brothers and sisters with whom they are ever so close, and you'll read about them in the next chapter and throughout this book. Meanwhile, it may be helpful to explore the world of mixed feelings.

One age-old question from parents—Why can't you be friends?—is a burden for Katie, who struggles with guilt over how she treated her younger sister. Thank heavens these warring sisters have two younger brothers, whom they adore. But their struggles are very old ones.

I'M NOT HER FRIEND

Katie can't be friends with her younger sister, because Katie spent their childhood being cruel to her. This sister came along when Katie was just eighteen months old, and Katie thinks that it was so hard to be nice to her little sister, because Katie was still a baby herself. At twenty-six, she struggles with guilt and distance from her sister. Katie's Just So Story took place at her sister's second birthday party. "There's a movie of her second birthday," Katie tells me. "She's opening up her presents and she gets a doll, and right away I try to take the doll and a stroller." The three-year-old Katie yelled, "I need it," and that's become sort of this family joke; they're always saying, "Katie *needs* it." Katie was crying hysterically and eventually the birthday girl said, "Okay, here Katie," and handed over the doll. Katie provides a commentary: "No matter what, I was the older sister she looked up to."

When she was young, Katie had some learning difficulties, which were exacerbated by the fact that her little sister was a natural student. In a family that prizes academic accomplishment, Katie felt that she was a loser, and she took it out on her sister. "I treated her terribly. Her friends would come over and I'd try to make them play with me instead of her, and then when we got older I was mean to them in the hallways at school." Katie stole her sister's things. She even took her clothes with her to college. Her mother found them when she was helping Katie unpack. And this continues. "She was staying in my apartment in the city with a friend and she called my mom and said, 'I found a pair of my sweatpants in Katie's drawer, and I found a sweatshirt with my friend's name on it.'" Katie makes no excuses for her behavior. "I'm the oldest and I'm bossy and controlling, that probably was very difficult for her. I always just felt that every-thing was unfair and that I wasn't good enough," she says.

She doesn't think they will ever be close. "I don't want to know about her personal life. I'm not interested in her sex life," Katie says. She doesn't want to be her sister's friend: "I feel incredibly guilty, but I can't help it." Katie and her sister have always pushed each other's buttons, but Katie is a good person and a very good sister to her brothers. She just couldn't bear the little rival who seemed to win every race, and so she acted like a child—mean, angry, jealous. That's what children do, but the younger ones may not understand why they have come in for such hostility. There are many ways of overcoming the initial disconnect between first and second children, but it is almost impossible for a younger child not to take the hostility and anger of the elder so personally.

Katie's story brings to mind all the second and third children who evoked the wrath of their siblings by zipping past them in sports, or school, or socially. I think of the little sisters and brothers who loved and admired the older ones, and who couldn't figure out what they had done wrong. My friend's older brother used to sing a little ditty he made up,

Maggie is a baby,
She can't walk,
She can't talk,
She cannot do anything.

To this day she can recall the tears that always flowed, even when she was a competent middle school kid, when he sang it. Perhaps this was his way of dealing with his "perfect" little sister and keeping her in her place—far enough behind him. She loved him and ran to him for help when she needed it and relied on his company when she was lonely. His anger didn't make sense until she understood the frustration of the first child when the competition begins to close the gap.

Because we know each other so well, our brothers and sisters can push our buttons in a way that friends and acquaintances cannot. The buttons were installed when we were very young. To some extent, pushing those buttons in our siblings is a way of staying close to them. The very ambivalence we experience is a link in the chain of our relationship. We sometimes have to be expert managers of ambivalence. Gloria has her stripes in that domain. She has issues with her older sister and worries endlessly about her three sparring twenty-something kids.

THE PAIN IN THE NECK

Gloria found a birthday card for her sister that she keeps in her desk drawer; she would never send it. The front of the card says,

A Sister is a Gift from God

Open up the card to see:

A Cruel, Vengeful, Punishing God
Birthday blessings on you

Gloria, the youngest of three girls, has dealt with mixed feelings toward her middle sister all her adult life. The oldest, with whom she is very close, is seven years her senior, and Gloria's middle sister is four years older. Their father committed suicide when Gloria was a baby. Her middle sister discovered him as she was searching for an old teddy bear in the attic. He was hanging from a rafter. She screamed and flew down the stairs to find their mother. Tragedy like this sets up rings of sorrow and pain through a family, and Gloria believes that the trauma marked the beginning of her middle sister's difficult personality. Gloria reminds herself of this when she is furious, and she feels empathy for her sister all over again. But fifty years is a long time, and Gloria can't always remember to forgive her sister. As a girl she always needed more attention and had to be the center of attention. Their mother protected her when her sisters got fed up with her. This mother had kept the family together too long to let it dissolve now.

One day, Gloria's mother took the difficult daughter to a fundraising luncheon, then came home and phoned Gloria to complain about this daughter's ingratitude and self-centeredness. The difficult sister knew she had been awful, so she stopped by to apologize to her mother. They were sitting on the couch, when her mother muttered, "Something is wrong," and keeled over, dead, right in front of Gloria's sister. This poor woman witnessed the death of both her parents, so it's no wonder she's always in a tizzy. But that doesn't make her easier to be around. Gloria had always contemplated cutting her sister off after their mother's death. Now she realizes that it's not a possibility. The bond they formed in childhood is too strong. When she gets annoyed, Gloria looks at the birthday card, and it still makes her smile. She knows she will never send it, and laughing over its message is her way of pushing her annoyance over to ambivalence.

———

Gloria's three children are in their twenties, and she frets because they don't get along. Nobody knows how better to push each other's buttons than this "ragtag group of siblings," as Andrea, twenty-three, the youngest, puts it. She spent nearly an hour telling me about her sister's annoying traits and her brother's infuriating personality.

Andrea and her siblings speak, Skype, or Gmail several times a week. They always fight when they are together, and they drive each other nuts. Andrea has been the mediator between her judgmental older sister and her opinionated older brother all their lives. These days, the brother worries both sisters. He likes to argue, and he needs to win. "He's hard to debate with, and it's hard for him to see the other side of issues," Andrea says. Her sister is "a grade A provoker of issues. If there's something she knows will push a button, she'll hit it." Andrea keeps her head down: "If they're fighting, I'm sitting in the middle, reading a book." Last week Andrea and her brother had an hour-long down-and-out argument over the pros and cons of infant vaccinations (neither of them is even in a relationship, much less thinking about having children). Her brother listed the risks of autism, and Andrea quoted the government's judgment that vaccinations do not cause autism. "My argument was, don't believe everything you read online," Andrea tells me. "And his was, you should read everything online."

This young man is stubborn. "We were on a family vacation, and one of my parents mentioned somebody winning the Nobel Prize." Her brother said, "Do you mean the Nobel Peace Prize?" And her mom replied, "No—there are Nobel Prizes for lots of things." He couldn't accept that: "But it's still the Nobel Peace Prize for Medicine, or the Nobel Peace Prize for Literature." The argument went on for twenty minutes. The brother would not give in. The next day he confessed, "I know that you guys were right yesterday, but I just couldn't let go."

This upsets the older sister, who remembers "the first time we had a real fight on the telephone; I just felt like he was being distant. I remember crying into all the tissues that I had, and just realizing, Wow, he's growing up, and we really just don't mesh that well."

Andrea's older sister is a detail-oriented and fastidious career woman. Like many first children, she needs to be in control. She's quick to judge—everybody but herself, says Andrea: "Our fights are always the same. She says something to me, and it always upsets me. She'll make a comment about a friend of mine, or judgments on people she doesn't know." It drives Andrea up the wall. And it can get ugly. "I was driving home from having dinner with my grandmother," Andrea recalls, "and we were fighting about God knows what. She scratched me while we were on the expressway, and it made my wheel swerve. I was so freaked out that she would touch me while I was driving on the expressway. I pulled over and I screamed at her until she cried." Her sister apologized and was repentant, but here is another quirk that bothers Andrea: her sister is slow to forgive but quick to expect forgiveness. "My mom told me that I sulk a lot," Andrea says, but she maintains that she has difficulty letting go of her anger because she knows that her sister will start up with her again in no time.

Listening to this litany of complaints and arguments, I concluded that their mother was right about her children's distance and scrapping. But her mom and I were both wrong. "Underneath everything, we love each other. And we do have fun together. The fighting is ten percent of our relationship," Andrea says.

When I ask the older sister, whom Andrea finds hypercritical, how she sees her little sister, I hear, "I just adore her. I respect her so much. She's gregarious. She makes friends easily. She's easygoing, relaxed. I'm anxious. It's hard for me to talk to new people. I'm in awe that she's able to pull all those things off." As for her pigheaded brother: "He's always argumentative, but he's also sweet. So after you get to the end of an argument, he'll step away, and he won't hold a grudge."

Gloria's three squabblers gathered at the bedside of their paternal grandmother when she was dying. Andrea tells the story: "The greater good was to make sure my grandma was comfortable, and we were all in the room and holding her hand and talking to her." Gloria was relieved to see her children stop fighting for those five days. Andrea remembers, "That was something we all saw the same way—we all have to be together now, and we can't fight. It's so petty when you're sitting with your grandma. I think that was a big shift for all of us."

Maybe the experience at their grandmother's bedside prompted them to plan their mother's fiftieth-birthday celebration, a surprise family weekend in New Orleans. The siblings had a great time coordinating everything in secret, and even gave one another code names. Andrea described the scene at baggage claim: their mom was watching the conveyer belt, looking for her suitcase. Suddenly, her three children appeared from behind the barriers. She was shocked, and she cried, they hugged, and the three kids managed not to fight for the whole weekend.

When I ask Andrea to compare her mother's sibling relationship with her own, she is clear: "I love my sister, and I like her, too. And I think that's what's missing from my mom and my aunt. I don't think they love each other, and they definitely don't like each other." I'm trying to reconcile this harsh evaluation as

Andrea continues, "But she's not going to let her go." Her mother's trials with the difficult sister are a warning to Andrea: "I look at my parents and their siblings, and I can't even imagine them being kids together, because they don't even have a relationship." They do, I want to tell Andrea, but it's complicated.

Listening to Gloria, I hear deep worry that her children will replicate her sibling relationships. Listening to her daughters, I hear a complex mix of annoyance and love, of frustration and admiration. This interweaving of positive and negative may not be ideal, but it is real, and there are good reasons for it to be more the rule than the exception. Sisters can snipe at each other all their lives and still be profoundly connected. Look at Renee and her sister.

THE BACK-SEAT SISTER

Renee and her younger sister have always been different. Renee, a successful businesswoman, knows what she wants and gets it. Her sister is the opposite—she has always been the good girl to whom things happen. They were not close as kids, and at the ages of sixty-nine and sixty-five, they are still stuck in conflict. They judge each other harshly. Renee thinks her little sister's misfortunes are due to bad judgment, and her sister resents Renee's judgmental attitude. These two sisters are so close that they can't stop fighting and don't stop talking. They even argue in front of their aging father and when their friends are around. But they won't give up on each other. Their tie is so strong and deep that it has lasted all their lives, with a few periods of silence for some relief from their constant bickering.

Renee trusts her decisions because they are backed by facts. The younger sister is vague, and she often lacks the courage to do what is best for herself. When her lifelong partner was diagnosed with a fatal cancer, Renee begged her sister to get him to rewrite his outdated will. He wouldn't discuss it ("You think I'm dying, don't you?"), so her sister let it go. The will left his entire estate to a wife he had divorced decades before. When her sister goes to Renee for sympathy, she gets a lecture. These women see life differently.

Renee is hurt when her sister doesn't take her advice, but it kills Renee when she doesn't even seek it. When her sister was moving to Renee's city, she went to a real estate agent instead of consulting Renee. "I was upset at that, really upset and insulted," Renee says. Renee thinks her sister bought the wrong house, and she cannot let it go. Renee admits that second-guessing is what she does, despite the fact that everybody tells her to stop. They all warn her, "She's the only sister you have."

Her sister takes revenge from time to time. When they were choosing a nursing home for their mother, the younger sister turned the whole thing over to Renee and told her to do whatever she thought was right. Renee spent lots of time and effort looking into it. She even hired an expert to help her find just the right place. Renee begged her sister to come and check it out. No, she wouldn't come—it was up to Renee. But of course when she finally did see the facility she told Renee she would never have chosen that place for their mother.

It has always been this way. When they were young, Renee was the rebel: "Every time my homeroom teacher said, 'Sit straight,' I sat sideways." Renee's little sister was the perfect one, doing beautifully in school, having lots of friends, and marrying young. Her life hasn't always gone well, so she thinks that Renee is the lucky one, even though Renee never married and has taken care of herself all her life.

Renee can't stop herself from sniping at her little sister. And yet they are very close. They live in the same city, and they speak all the time. Recently Renee's sister showed some spunk—a rare quality, in Renee's eyes. She was in therapy with a person she didn't much care for, and when the therapist suggested that she do something assertive for herself, the sister said, "Okay, I'm quitting therapy with you!" Renee was thrilled, and she is happy that her sister has decided to join her church, which is more liberal than the suburban congregation where her sister lives.

Renee's sister is also joining her choir. It could be that singing together will help them achieve a harmony of spirit. I don't know if this experience will curb Renee's need to carp and her sister's love of quiet revenge, but it might be a start. What begins in church might spread to other aspects of their world. These women have always needed each other; what they need now is a key in which they can find a bit of harmony.

There's a myth out there that good relations between brothers and sisters do not include conflict, annoyance, differences, or any other combination of mixed feelings. That is a destructive myth, because it makes people doubt the strength of their connection with their siblings. I thought that a short list of misgivings and ambivalences might make people feel better about themselves, their siblings, and the future. This list is not complete. Feel free to add to it.

Their quirks drive us nuts.
We want them to reflect well on us.
We can't understand why we differ in so many important ways.

We feel responsible for their failings.

We find even the ones we love deeply annoying at times.

We can be profoundly hurt and still worry about them.

When something good happens to one of them, joy can be mixed with jealousy.

When bad things happen, we sometimes feel that they got what they deserved.

It kills us when we don't want to be generous or loving to them.

It hurts our feelings terribly when they aren't sufficiently grateful.

We yearn to be close but don't know where to begin.

We feel guilty about our failures, and we long to be better siblings.

Mixed feelings are the raw materials of sibling relationships (perhaps of all relationships), and one of our jobs is to find a balance of positive and negative that we can live with. Some brothers and sisters are happy being Wedding and Wake siblings; they get together only on big family occasions. They greet each other with enthusiasm and part with relief. That's fine. Others speak on the phone from time to time, keeping in touch without a strong connection. That's fine. Some brothers and sisters find that they are just too abrasive with each other to be in touch at all. That's fine, too, although it is often accompanied by guilt and sorrow.

Many close brothers and sisters, who enjoy a loving and flexible bond, work at it. And then, of course, there are brothers and sisters who are close without effort, who started out with an affinity. If you are one of them, you'll recognize yourself in the next chapter.

4

LOOKING FOR LOVE
IN ALL THE RIGHT PLACES

People with ambivalent feelings toward their siblings have a hard time believing brothers and sisters when they say they are each other's best friends. Just recently a friend took me aside, tilted her head toward mine, and quietly asked if I had really found any brothers and sisters with that "special" relationship. I have: brothers and sisters whose connection is strong, pervaded by mutual acceptance and appreciation. They love to be in each other's company and they make each other happy. The sense of responsibility they bear is a light load for them, and no sacrifice feels too great.

After reading about nursery battles and enduring ambivalence, it is important to know that loving, caring, and close brothers and sisters are all around us. They come in many different family constellations and they exhibit love and loyalty, respect and responsibility. What makes these different from the other relationships? The answer seems to be connection, a deep and powerful empathy and mutual respect. Brothers and sisters who enjoy this connection confide in each other with confidence, laugh at themselves and each other, and celebrate their relaxed intimacy. Their trust in each other's ability to offer acceptance makes it easy to communicate differences as well as similarities. They shrug off actions and habits that might drive other siblings crazy.

Some of these people didn't get along as children; others loved each other at first sight. Some grew up in easy families; others survived difficult childhoods. Not every moment of these close relationships was harmonious, mind you. There were arguments and disappointments, but something allowed the difficulties to dissolve over time, leaving a fierce sense of commitment and a residue of intimacy and love. Even when they disagreed and fought and got angry, there was no question about their affection.

Here are two brothers who just love each other—who experienced the childhood scuffles and jealousies, but whose affinity for each other trumps everything else. It began on the day the newborn little brother came home from the hospital and has gotten better ever since.

PEAS IN A POD

"We definitely always felt like we were lucky to be brothers."
—Kenneth

Kenneth and his brother have always been close. Kenneth recently relocated from his longtime home in Chicago to Minneapolis, where his brother lives. They wanted to live in the same city. Kenneth, twenty-nine, was three years old when his little brother arrived. "I was so excited when he was born," Kenneth says. "My aunt from California had come in to stay with me, and I still have memories of sitting on the stairs by the front door and having her say, 'He's not coming home yet; it's going to be a couple of hours.' His birthday's in January, so it was very cold out and every time the door opened and I peeked out, I remember the air on my face, it was that kind of excitement."

It is not unusual for the first child to be excited about the arrival of the new baby, but most three-year-olds are disappointed when they don't get an instant playmate and are forced to share their parents' attention. Kenneth and his brother did the usual fighting and pummeling, but hard feelings didn't last. They spent weekends and holidays at the home of their maternal grandparents, whom the boys adored. This Italian Catholic couple accepted their Jewish grandsons completely, and that included helping Grandma in the kitchen. Kenneth says, "My brother and I never had to figure out how to fend for ourselves because we knew what we were doing in the kitchen—I can make an incredible pasta."

Of course, Kenneth's little brother got under his skin. Kenneth's first Just So Story takes place in the back seat of the family car. "The one thing that really bothered me was his tendency to snore. When we were driving in the car for a long distance, he would figure out a way where his head would drop on my shoulder when he knew that he was going to snore. I would complain, 'Mom! He's snoring.'" I can feel the annoyance running through Kenneth's body, but I can also hear the laughter in his voice.

On the car trips, instead of competing about how many cows, horses, red barns, or silos they could sight, these brothers were given scavenger-hunt type games, Kenneth tells me. "They always involved us having to work together, so I was writing things down or he was telling me what to look for. We were a team, and it helped us entertain each other."

The boys were not so close in the years when his brother was playing high school basketball, but by the time both brothers were in college, they were making the effort to stay connected. They just like each other and are happy to be together.

When their mother recently took a trip to Florida, the brothers played tag team with their dad, to make sure he was okay. Kenneth is relieved to know that he won't be left alone to care for their parents when they get old. I asked Kenneth what he might say if he were to make a toast at his brother's wedding. Here's what Kenneth offered: "I think it'd be important for them to know about how compassionate he is, how sensitive he is, because those are characteristics people wouldn't think he has."

Kenneth's brother has a girlfriend, the only child of only children, who is overwhelmed at Kenneth's family gatherings—too many people, too much food and noise. Kenneth has tried the hardest of any family member to get along with her, because he's never going to let his brother drift away from him. Their degree of closeness is unusual, and Kenneth knows it. In fact, he offered to be interviewed because of that, saying, "I have an odd relationship with my brother because we like each other."

Kenneth has always loved and enjoyed his little brother, and that has made their connection easy. Not so with Amanda, who only discovered her little sister in a way that many specially loving siblings do, in her first year of college.

OPPOSITES ATTRACT

"We both always say that if we weren't related, we would never be friends."
—Amanda

Nearly six feet tall, blond, and blue-eyed, with a pale oval face that is just short of perfection, Amanda is beautiful. But even when she walks straight across a room, it's as if she's leaning on the wall—she doesn't want to draw attention to herself.

This has always been Amanda's way. The elder of two girls, as a child she was "hiding behind my father, shy." Studious and serious, Amanda excelled at school but didn't do so well with her classmates. Her younger sister, who arrived when Amanda was eighteen months old, is her opposite. She was never a grind; this outgoing, athletic girl was always at ease socially and very popular. She took risks and didn't consider the consequences—she just wanted to have fun. "Rather than having sibling rivalry, I embarrassed her because she had to follow the geek. I was dorky and super quiet and reserved," Amanda says. Close in age, close in looks, these girls had little in common.

Amanda admits that she wasn't especially nice to her little sister. She was jealous of her ability to make friends, her effortless sense of style, and her ease with being at the center of things. "We used to argue all the time over the phone. My parents set a rule that we could use the phone for twenty minutes at a time. I would always make her get off the phone in twenty minutes. She's like, 'Yes, but you don't have anyone to call.' I was like, 'Yes, I do,' and I really didn't, but I would make her get off just because I wanted my twenty minutes. She could have been on the phone all night."

Amanda tells me that people always wonder, "How did you and your sister turn out so different?" Amanda is conservative and admits that she was a highly judgmental teenager. She never drank or smoked—anything—she was always neat, and she finished her assignments early and wouldn't dream of breaking a rule. Her sister was the opposite. She would leave cigarette butts in their bathroom when her friends came over. Not Amanda; not Miss Perfect. Of course, she didn't have friends who came over, either. Amanda never approved of her sister's ways.

Amanda looked forward to college, because in college intelligence and hard work would be valued, and she wouldn't feel so geeky and dorky. Unfortunately, she landed at a drinking school. Like so many freshman girls these days, she was overwhelmed by the amount of casual sex, alcohol, and drugs that went down every day and night—not just on weekends. The dorm was noisy 24-7, she couldn't find friends, and she hated being there. By Thanksgiving, Amanda was ready to drop out.

It pained her parents to see their daughter so unhappy, and they would have let her leave school, but not her little sister. "You have to stay," she told Amanda. "If you don't you won't finish college in four years." I wonder where her caring sister's attitude came from. Perhaps Amanda wasn't as mean as she thinks she was.

Amanda knew her sister was right, and she didn't want to cause her parents any added tuition expense, but she didn't see how she could survive. Amanda underestimated her support system. Her sister talked her through the rest of the year. "Just stick it out, and then you can transfer at the end of the year," she would say on the phone. Amanda tells me, "My parents said she would come home at night—she was involved in three sports and academically and everything else—and be so tired, but I would call in tears, bawling, so she'd spend an hour or more on the phone with me." Amanda takes a deep breath. "That year totally changed our relationship."

Amanda came home that spring and spent her sophomore year commuting to a nearby college. Her little sister was now a senior in high school and active in sports. Amanda decided to cheer her on, as much for running up and down the hockey field as for scoring a goal. If her freshman year of college was the year when Amanda discovered she could depend on her sister, the next year she became her little sister's biggest fan.

When it came time to choose a college for her last two years, Amanda had an idea. Why not go to the same school? Amanda would have her sister's support, and her sister would have a cheerleader. That's what they did, one as a freshman and the other as a junior. "At the end of high school, I never would have said that," Amanda admits. What a change these two years had made.

It was a good decision. They had a ball. "Everybody thought we were twins. We ate every single meal together, and everything we did on the weekends was together." Amanda never stopped her fan's life: "She played on a pickup team. It wasn't even intramural, and I went to every pickup team game and sat there on the gym floor."

Still, the sisters didn't merge—they continued to make very different choices. After college, they took vacations together. Amanda's best friend (an Amanda clone) has a younger sister who is also a free spirit, so she invited them to come along. It was good, because nobody felt abandoned. "The four of us would go away every summer. And the house would be filled with pot smoke and they'd all be drunk, and I'd be sitting out on the stoop," Amanda says. But she wasn't alone—she had her best friend sitting on the sidewalk beside her.

In some families, such important cultural and moral differences would create a wide gulf, expressed in the question, How come we are so different? In Amanda's case, the question is asked in wonder: How can we be so different and yet so close? This is one of the great benefits of having siblings—you can be surprised when the people you weren't nice to step up to help. You may learn that being different isn't necessarily being wrong, and that needing something from a former enemy doesn't always end in disappointment.

Amanda and I met soon after her sister's wedding. They'd even spoken on her honeymoon, she told me. Her phone rang every day. "She'd be like, 'He's in the shower. We have five minutes.' Or, 'He went to golf. We have five minutes.'" People at work wondered, "Why is your sister calling you from her honeymoon?" Amanda had the answer: "Because we can't go that long without talking." Now, "she calls me every morning on her way into work, and that's like our fifteen minutes each morning."

They don't expect to agree on everything, "We're still very different," Amanda concedes. "I'm way more conservative, but not as conservative as I was, and she's still way more free-spirited, but not as free-spirited. But we'll never meet in the middle." This seems fine with both of them. At the wedding, their grandfather worried that their relationship might change with one of them married. Amanda shrugs off that concern. The couple had been living together for eight years (something Amanda would never dream of doing), and that hadn't separated the sisters. Her brother-in-law is not jealous of the sisters' closeness. Amanda gets quiet, and then she says, "We've often talked about, 'What would we do if something happened to one of us?' She's like, 'It would be worse than something happening to him, it would be worse than something happening to Mom or Dad.' I truly don't know how we would function without each other."

I hope the stories of these two sets of siblings do not make their relationships sound too good to be true. There have been bumps and there will be more, because life always deals out surprises that stress even the closest relationships. Kenneth may find it not so easy to deal with his brother's wife and her family, and Amanda and her sister may find it difficult to maintain their closeness when their lives get more complicated. But I think that having developed their connection, and enjoyed its benefits, these teams of nonrivals will work hard to maintain a degree of closeness and commitment.

There's another team of siblings that seems to beat the odds against ambivalence and distance. A woman I know told me that her younger brother "taught me the meaning of unadulterated love." She is not unusual. Some older sisters care for their younger brothers with a fierce loyalty and unalloyed protectiveness. These older sisters loved their younger brother, took care of him—some say, "I raised him"—and will look after him forever.

Men with this kind of sister should wear a T-shirt that says "Lucky Guy." Whatever happens, they have someone looking out for them—for the rest of their lives. These women have a concern for their brothers that is both sisterly and motherly. They accept their brothers' weaknesses and are forgiving. They feel guilty about what they haven't done for them, and are alert on their behalf. Necessity played a role in Gina's lifelong commitment to her little brother, but her love for him began long before adversity set in.

LUCKY GUY

Gina was eight years old when her brother was born, and she immediately adored him. She still does. A brilliant and eccentric kid, her brother was a superb student, a musical prodigy, and a boy who wouldn't eat two peas if they touched each other on the plate. When he was a teenager, their father died. Gina had recently married, so she and her husband moved right into the parental role (their mother never recovered from her husband's death). The brother was, for all his prodigious talents, childlike. They drove him to the Big Ten university where he had a scholarship and unpacked his room for him. The next summer, Gina tells me, "We had rented a house on the lake, and I was pregnant. He came out with almost no luggage, and he looked at my husband's feet. He was wearing flip-flops. 'Can I have those?' And my husband took the flip-flops off his feet and gave them to him." Carry the furniture up the stairs, unpack the books, watch your husband give him flip-flops off his feet—never mind, he's my brother.

The serious mental breakdowns began when her brother was a college sophomore, and he had to drop out of school to enter a psychiatric hospital. For a year he lived as an outpatient while they worked on his medication. His outbreaks after that were sporadic. "I was very worried about him all the time," Gina says. "His first breakdown was in April, and every time April rolled around, the cruelest month, I would start to get anxious." Medication helped, but mental illness puts everybody on an emotional roller coaster. Soon after their mother died, he went off his meds, and things began to fall apart again.

Gina got a call. He was at a conference in Seattle, and he'd thrown all the furniture into the pool. "I flew out with a friend of his who was a flying phobic; the guy is doing white knuckles on the plane. We bailed him out of the jail with a couple of shotfuls of his meds, and we took two rooms in a motel. His friend and I are in one room. Suddenly he comes in naked, luridly psychotic, and we had to hospitalize him."

Gina always thought of herself as the "normal one," not nearly as gifted as her brother, who by the time of this episode had a solid career as a computer scientist. She wasn't jealous of his talents, in part because as a child he felt that his gifts were a burden, but mostly because she wasn't in competition with him—she loved him and she would care for him.

Over the years he married and had children. When he flipped out, his wife would call Gina to fly out and help take care of her crazy husband, and Gina did—except for once. He was flagrantly psychotic again. Gina's sister-in-law wanted her to drop everything. But Gina was on vacation, far away from civilization and airplanes, and she knew that she couldn't do her brother any good just by being there; he needed to be hospitalized. Gina offered to send money and make the relevant phone calls, but this one time she couldn't leave her family. Eventually her brother went back on his meds, and things calmed down. To this day Gina blames herself for not going to her brother's aid. His wife isn't forgiving, either. They had it out, but the guilt lingers, as does her sister-in-law's resentment.

Gina still feels bad about this, despite having been an amazing sister. In addition to bailing her brother out of his crises, she has set up small trust funds for his children's educations (which she cannot afford); she sends the kids generous presents, and she looks for opportunities to help them out. Gina is her brother's keeper. She does it without anger, and she loves him as much as she did when he was a baby. Theirs has not been a very mutual relationship until recently. Gina tells me that her brother has been of help to her, monitoring the moods of a dear friend who has a similar chemical disturbance, and she is grateful.

This good big sister continues to try to repair her brother's life. "The week after my father died," she relates, "my cousin, the daughter of my aunt, was getting married. My mother was out of it and decided to give them our piano as a wedding present, which my brother, who is a musical prodigy, still played. And she did. How crazy is that?" Her brother never played piano again.

"Now he was turning fifty," she continues. Gina flew out to celebrate the birthday. Her nephew picked her up at the airport, and she hid in the back of her nephew's car on the way to the party. She appeared just in time to see the look on her brother's face when he noticed the piano sitting in his living room—a gift from his sister.

I asked Gina to help me understand what made her want to be such a good sister, and affinity is the major factor. But she also had a model in her mother's sister, Aunt Bertha. A successful businesswoman, she had a popular dress shop in the 1950s, and when Gina's father died, she gave her mother work there. She was always generous to Gina and her brother, and she was also a lot of fun. I think Gina was happy to find that she could be a little like Aunt Bertha.

Gina and her brother didn't have to work through sibling

rivalry—they were so far apart in age, and their talents were so different. The difference between her situation and her brother's was a blessing. But the real blessing was Gina's character—her continuing commitment to care for her younger brother and her ability to do it with love. Gina rose to the occasion. This is one of the great opportunities siblings are given: to find their more accepting selves, their loving side, and their sense of heightened responsibility at a young age.

There is a mythic quality to the courage and energy of the child who rises to the occasion and takes care of the other children. These kids are heroes in the sagas of their families. Think of the era before antibiotics, when so many mothers died in childbirth, leaving a brood of little ones for the oldest to bring up. Consider our pioneer families, who could not have settled the West without the participation of the older children to herd the tots as well as the farm animals, to wash and scold, feed and nurture them while the parents struggled to survive. Remember the immigrant families whose elder children went to school, learned the language, translated the culture for the greenhorn parents, and then quit school to support their families. These keepers of the keys not only provided for their siblings but also exemplified a sense of mission and rightness for the family. Many of them remain dedicated caregivers all their lives, but they are often unable to get their own needs satisfied. The younger siblings sometimes carry resentment toward the bossy sister or brother, and there is no way under heaven or on earth for the keeper of the keys to get sufficient gratitude. We might think of this as an example of the ironic statement "No good deed goes unpunished," but something much deeper is operating here: it's called survival, and even though the surface is pockmarked with conflict, love, loyalty, and gratitude are always just below. The pull and push of gratitude and annoyance, autonomy and dependence roils these siblings for life. But they know, and everybody around them knows, the incredible strength of their bond.

ROSIE AND HER SISTERS

My first experience with a keeper of the keys came very early. She was my mother, who was carried through Ellis Island, an infant in her mother's arms. For six years, they struggled alone on New York's Lower East Side. Then my grandfather arrived. He labored as a pieceworker, pedaling the sewing machine from dawn to dusk, earning a penny for a pair of pants. It must have been terribly wrenching for this bright and imperious six-year-old when her father showed up and diverted her mother's attention. Rosie never got along with her father, and he couldn't bear his "American" daughter, who spoke and read English, and who knew her way around.

Then came the babies. The first sister, their father's favorite, was born less than a year after he arrived. The rest came a year apart. Some died as infants, including a pair of twins who did not survive the flu epidemic of 1918. Neither did Rosie's mother, who preceded her father to the grave by a year. My mother always said her father died of a broken heart. The only kind words he had for her came on his deathbed, when he praised her for taking care of him and her four sisters, saying, "Rosie, you've been a good daughter."

Thrust at the age of seventeen into the role of Little Mother (the youngest sister was three years old), Rosie battled the authorities who wanted to adopt out "the girls," as they were known all their lives. My mother won, and she raised them herself, shuttling from school to work, to the stores for food, to home, cleaning, cooking their meals, and sewing their clothes. They walked for miles from their tenement apartment to a fine New York City public school, and when the soles of their shoes wore out, she cut cardboard pieces to replace the leather. When she married my father, six years later, he took them all in. That was my mother's dowry: four little girls to raise and educate.

They stayed close all their lives. My brother and I loved the Aunts (now there were three) more than anybody in the world. The best aunt, who was the youngest, lived with us when I was a baby, and she was my protector. Their father's favorite, the first daughter born in America, was the nearest thing we ever saw to a miser. My brother loved her most of all, and she would bring him extremely simple presents. The other aunts lavished much of their meager earnings on gifts. But my brother would carry around a new pair of socks from Aunt Jeanette and leave the fancy set of blocks in the box. This made the generous sisters furious.

The most outspoken of the sisters married and moved away, where she and her husband had a child and a full life. As they got older, the other two lived within a block of my parents. They spoke every day, and the aunts ate dinner at my house most nights. The miser used to sneak leftovers home, which enraged my father; my mother didn't care. The angel aunt worked for my mother (it was a way for my parents to support her), so that she could send her smart son to a special high school for gifted kids.

It was not possible for the sisters to remain as docile as my mother expected. Resentment was always in the air. My mother was generous and militant. Her temper, which was an excellent way to suppress dissent when they were small, never dissipated. Sometimes "the girls" tried to push back, but they always gave in. When the aunts came for a fried chicken dinner, a big platter would appear, and my mother would tell each sister which piece to take. She didn't intend to be pushy; she just knew what was best for them, down to the choice of dark or light meat.

My husband and I would visit from out of town, and each of the aunts would take me aside and complain. Whispering behind one another's back and grousing, rolling their eyes and stalking out of the room—no sisters could be closer than those three. The energy they generated could have powered a city. One friend called them the Three Fates; another dubbed them the Three Weird Sisters. Whatever you call them, they kept one another going. I realized the full power of their intensity when my mother died. I expected my father to follow her within a couple of years—and he did. But I was surprised that the two closest sisters, seven and thirteen years younger than my mother, died soon after my father. The only sister who survived was the one who had moved away. Her ability to live without my mother's attention kept her going for another decade.

The heroic retelling of my mother's exploits, their childhood poverty and their tribulations, was part of my childhood. When I was a little girl, I used to run out of the room in tears because the stories made me so sad. The adults would call me back and tell me not to cry, that everything had turned out fine. They were right, but so was I. The suffering was real. Years later, my cousin and I discussed the shadow cast on the lives of our mothers by the death of their parents when they were so young. We agreed that, because of what they suffered, each of them was diminished, and it took all four sisters to make one regular person: my mother was ambition and energy, the good aunt was kindness and self-sacrifice, the miser was warped by all that had befallen them, and the fighter was the honest one. Four sisters, fighting, loving, and surviving.

The keeper of the keys develops a heightened sense of responsibility that never abates, and much of his or her identity is based on being generous and selfless. It's amazing how kids rise to the occasion and push themselves far beyond what they thought possible. They are rightfully proud of their accomplishments, and they never lose the sense that they must care for their siblings.

I'm beginning to think that when one of the siblings takes over the brothers and sisters, a pattern of interactions specific to this particular constellation takes place. It's as if the movements of the stars in the family are set early. There's always one sibling who plays the rebel, and another who is the helper in chief. The others are arrayed in various degrees of gratitude and resentment, based on the way in which the keeper of the keys wielded authority and on the connections among the others. Although the strife lasts for life, so does the depth of love and dependence, whether it is expressed through joy, annoyance, or everything in between.

Listening to these close brothers and sisters, I keep picturing a magic overcoat—perhaps I have read too much Harry Potter.

But bear with me for a moment. Imagine a garment that brothers and sisters can share, big enough for all of them and supplying what they need: security, comfort, warmth, and sustenance. As they grow, the dimensions of the overcoat change, and when they are apart, it stretches. Brothers and sisters who live in this coat know how lucky they are, and if there is a worn place or a hole, they rush to mend it. I think of a classic children's book, *Joseph Had a Little Overcoat*. In that book the old overcoat progressively wears out and is turned into a smaller and smaller object, ending in a button. Once Joseph's button wears out, he makes a story out of it. I love the book and have read it many times to my grandson. But now I am thinking that perhaps close brothers and sisters start with the story, and then between or among them, create the button, which grows into the handkerchief, which they build into a scarf, which they make into a vest, which then, over time and through loving acts, turns into their magic overcoat. Nothing valuable is easy. The brothers and sisters in this chapter know how lucky they are—and they are mindful of the garment they have created together.

Part 2

LIFE'S COURSE

5

GRAVITY SHIFTS

The culture is full of books and movies about how hard it is for fathers to give their daughters away in marriage. And when a mother sighs, "I'm not losing a son, I'm gaining a daughter," we hear the prayer that lies behind her words. No such phrase expresses how people feel when a brother or sister gets married, except for one of the most moving moments at a wedding party: the toast from the best man or the maid of honor. Think about the weddings you've attended, and the brothers and sisters you've heard. The speech usually begins with shared childhood memories of the silly things they did together. Then come brave and loving acts that attest to the bride or groom's virtues, followed by warm words of welcome to the newcomer. Finally the speaker entrusts the beloved sibling to the new spouse. These words convey pride and love, combined with a poignant good-bye. I always get teary at that moment, and people often find it moving—we all know what it feels like to give a brother or a sister away, even if it's temporary. When the happy couple returns from their honeymoon, the work of the brothers and sisters begins in earnest. It goes on for a lifetime, and it sometimes feels like heavy lifting.

A sister tells me how angry she is at her brother's wife for pulling him away from the family, and for being jealous of their time together. "He only calls me from the car on his way to work," she complains. Should she blame her brother or his wife?

A man tells me that his sister-in-law has always been negative, and wouldn't even eat the food the brothers cooked together when he visited. What is that about?

I know a sister who secretly thinks her brother should take his wife's last name—he seems to have married her family and divorced his own. What's going on here?

A friend is dumbstruck by her brother's decisions about where to live, how to spend his money, and when to see his own children and grandchildren—she blames the wife. Is she right?

Two women tell me that they were devastated to learn that their sister disappeared after she married because her husband was jealous of her closeness to the family. Why did they have to wait for the divorce to learn this?

We have no say over our brother or sister's choice of mate, which is just as well. But we often feel helpless when the newcomer doesn't get along, doesn't like the family, and pulls our sibling away. This is hard for parents, but I think it's even more of a problem for brothers and sisters, because they feel powerless to counter a dynamic they usually did not create. Most people expect the wife to stay close to her family, moving her husband into its orbit. This is very hard on a man's siblings, who usually don't think they have the right to pull their brother back, and would not know how to do it, anyway. Over time, early patterns are set in stone. This can be a source of sorrow for siblings, who may realize how much they miss each other.

Even if everybody tries hard to get along, the family dynamic changes. It has to. New sensibilities and sensitivities are introduced. Family styles may clash. A quiet woman coming into a boisterous family may feel overwhelmed. She may not care for the food or the manners of her husband's family. The brothers and sisters may in turn find her cold and withholding, mistaking style for substance. Even if they were always close, they hesitate to criticize, and there isn't as much time to talk anymore—loss upon loss for siblings. Brothers and sisters may believe that their sibling isn't being treated as well as he or she deserves—here comes another reason for distance. It goes on for life, and conquering this centrifugal pull away is often so hard that people give up.

I know a woman whose brother married three times. The first wife was close to her mother, but the families were all great friends, and things were easy. Then came the divorce. Old friendships disappeared in the face of rage, and everybody suffered. When he married a woman who didn't care for his family, he withdrew. This man was lucky the third time when he married a woman who likes them, and the siblings are close again. She and her sisters pray that this marriage will last. As if what they felt mattered!

Keeping up the old closeness under new circumstances takes more than courage and tact. It takes energy and commitment.

Even inconsequential differences can be hard to overcome. Wendy, a single woman in her late twenties, has always been extremely close to her brother. He recently married and moved near his wife's family. Wendy misses him. She knows how important it is to bond with her new sister-in-law. Wendy doesn't dissemble, so it is hard for her to be less than open. But when she disagrees with her brother's wife, her brother gets tense. For now, honesty is at war with tact.

WENDY TALKS TO HERSELF

We are sitting in a beautiful little garden on New York's Upper West Side, on a soft spring day. The tulips come in a magnificent array of colors, and the navy blue irises are tall and frilly. A slender young woman with reddish-brown hair cut to her jawline, Wendy describes how much she loves her brother. She is soft-spoken and ducks her head as she describes the obstacles she is doing her best to overcome.

Wendy and her little brother have always been close. They share a deep connection with and sympathy for each other. Wendy says, "I remember going to seek him out on the playground during recess, especially in first grade, making sure he was okay. Then, when he was in first grade and I was in third grade, the class bully was picking on me and my brother beat him up! He was two years littler, and just smacked the heck out of this guy." Wendy treasures the strength of their connection.

Wendy has always taken to heart her mother's maxim "You two are all you'll have," and she knows that her brother's wife is now part of the equation. I hear a wistful undertone in Wendy's voice. The changes that have taken place since her brother got married bother her, and she is disappointed in her-self for being resentful. When he moved away to live in his wife's hometown, Wendy was not happy. "I groused when they were moving," she says. The two-hour drive, although some-times arduous, is not the problem. It's the difference from Wendy's expectations that jars her. Wendy always thought that she and her brother would live near each other, just like her mother and her aunts and uncles—within her family's orbit. Wendy comforts herself with one idea, though: "I keep on reminding myself that at least she's not from Seattle!"

"What's she like?" I ask. "She's lovely. She's very different from me, and that took the biggest adjustment." "Tell me about it." "Well, I didn't expect my brother to marry someone who was exactly like me, but we have very different political views. She's much more conservative than I am. In the grand scheme of things, it's not a big deal, but it took me by surprise." Differ-ences in religion and politics can drive wedges between sib-lings. Wendy confides, "I always think that we could talk about it and you can disagree, but I could see my brother tense up, because he wants everyone to get along. So we try to avoid it." Not saying what she thinks keeps Wendy from being genuine, which for her is a central component of intimacy. Today, in the warm sunlight, she says that she has been relaxing into their differences just a bit: "If I'm sitting around reading the newspa-per, I purposely don't censor myself anymore, because I figure at this point she knows that she's my family, I love her." Wendy is mindful of sensitivities, and she is watchful. "I don't go over-board," she says.

One of the teachings of this altered relationship is that the new relative isn't automatically a member of the family—it takes time. Wendy has learned that personality differences require careful attention. "She's much more reserved, and that took me aback. I think I'm always being on my best behavior, and she is on her very best behavior." I imagine that Wendy's visits could be trying for the newlyweds. Picture Wendy relaxing into a big chair in a neat suburban house, her ankles crossed on the cocktail table, reading the paper and responding to the news with excitement or annoyance. Imagine her brother hunching up his shoulders in concern.

It's hard for a sister to criticize the new wife, but a lot easier for the new wife to complain about her husband's sister. Wendy's brother is fortunate that his sister senses his discomfort and responds by backing off. This good sister is at work resetting her expectations. "They still don't do things the way I would do them, but I realize that it doesn't really matter," she says. It would be very easy for Wendy to take umbrage at her sister-in-law's formality and to make a big deal about their religious and political differences. But Wendy says, "I also keep them in perspective and I'm careful about who I grouse to." She uses her friends and her mother as sounding boards, so her "grouses" won't get back to her brother. And she takes the long view: "I think it's just making a decision that this relationship is important to you and is the relationship that's going to last your entire life, and you just do the best you can."

Wendy is working diligently to avoid putting her brother in the middle. I hope his wife is working at it too, because her husband loves his sister. The wife would be wise to support this relationship. He'll be happier, and Wendy may even come to her aid in unexpected ways.

———

Sally's brother is not so lucky. His sister and his wife have been fighting over him all his life, and he has done his best to keep them both happy. Now his efforts have failed—the balancing act of a lifetime fell apart after their father died. Sally blames her brother's wife for everything that has gone wrong. She sees no responsibility for herself, or her brother, in this. I don't know Sally's sister-in-law, but I suspect that the tie between her husband and his sister has been a thorn in her side for many years.

WINNER TAKE ALL

It began badly, over thirty years ago. When Nathan presented his fiancée to his parents, they went ballistic—she wasn't Jewish, and that was that. They refused to attend the wedding, and for years they didn't speak. This is an explosive family, where yelling is the norm and violent feelings are expressed regularly. The young woman, coming from a polite Catholic family, disliked all of Sally's kin from Day One. Even though Sally was the only family member to attend the wedding, the bride resented her, too. She made no distinctions among her husband's intense relatives. The relationship between the women never "took." Sally hoped that because she sided with this woman and attended the wedding, she would be able to maintain a close relationship with her brother. That did not happen, to Sally's astonishment. Sally cared for Nathan in that big-sister, little-brother way when they were kids, and when they were both unmarried and living in the same city, they spent a lot of time together—which, Sally reports, was a happy time for her: "We've always had a bond."

Sally says her sister-in-law is self-centered, inflexible, and demanding. When Nathan added fuel to the fire by confiding problems with his wife, Sally became convinced that her brother would be happier divorced from this woman. She knows, she says, that "he's not going to do it. I would try to talk to him, and I felt horrible being in a position of being the heavy." Nobody wants to be in that position—there is a steep price to be paid for coming between a man and his wife, no matter how miserable they seem. "You don't know how many tears I've shed about it over the years," she says.

Nathan's wife could have been suspicious of Sally; the brother and sister spoke all the time. When the wife objected to their lengthy telephone conversations, Nathan arranged for Sally to call him late at night, after his wife was asleep. This subterfuge may not have worked. You don't have to be fully awake to notice when the phone rings once and is instantly picked up. "And then for a while," Sally tells me, "he was calling me at my office on an afternoon when he knew she wasn't going to be home. It was like we were having an affair."

So when the tension between the women finally erupted into a fight (it was over a trifle, as most of these fights are), a curtain of silence fell between sister and brother. This rift was too painful for Sally. "I really worked on myself spiritually and wrote her a note and said, If I've done anything to offend you, I apologize." Nice. But she couldn't leave it at that, adding, "Try to remember the times when you called on me for help." The sister-in-law went ballistic, responding with a letter that said, "I don't want to have a relationship with you." Then, complete silence.

Nathan phoned several months later, to try to reconnect, but

Sally told him, "I've been robbed of my brother." Nathan then invited Sally for a weekend visit and arranged for his wife to be away at their beach house. Sally smiles, "We had a really nice time and I thought, Oh, he's back. He's back."

Then their father died. But when Nathan mentioned that his wife and daughter were coming to the funeral, Sally made what may have been the mistake of her life. "Nathan," she said, "I want to have time alone with you." There was a long silence on the other end of the phoneline. Nathan came alone. "That was good," Sally says. "He cried and he hugged me and he said he had missed me and he said he never wanted this to happen between us again." After the funeral, to her amazement, Sally stopped hearing from her brother. When she called, Nathan responded in a monotone. He couldn't wait to hang up. Sally may have won that battle, but she lost the war. Long estranged from her other brother, divorced, and with no children, she is profoundly alone. "When 9/11 happened," she says, "nobody called to see if I was okay."

They run into each other at family events. When they recently met at a cousin's wedding, Nathan's wife was polite: "Hello, Sally, nice to see you." It wasn't nice for Sally. She has lost her brother for good. Sally would rewind this film if she could. But there was nothing she could do about her parents' outrage at their son's choice of wife. And she comes from a family where the choice was always clear: My way or the highway. Sally and her brother struggled for decades seeking the middle path, tipping back and forth between closeness and distance. In the end, just as they were embarking on the time in life when they had no parents left, Sally put Nathan on the spot. He finally ran out of options, and the balancing act was over. Perhaps he is relieved that he no longer needs to make choices between the warring women in his life. But I bet there's a part of Nathan that longs for his big sister, to confide in, and also to comfort.

In the course of my travels I did meet a man who answered the question, Where have all our brothers gone? Anthony went over to his wife's family, and for good reason, he thinks. His wife has a terrific relationship with her sister, and he loves his in-laws. His sister-in-law and her husband have gone out of their way to share their children with Anthony and his wife, who do not plan to have kids of their own. Anthony's father died when he was eight years old; his wife's father has become a loving surrogate dad, and his mother-in-law is just an easy person to be around.

On the other hand, his sister is married to a man who doesn't bother to greet him and his wife when they arrive, after a two-hour drive. Anthony's wife is used to a more polite way of behaving, and her feelings get hurt. His sister has never left her children with the couple, and Anthony and his wife watch in anger as his sister and her sluggard husband mooch off his widowed mother. His mother doesn't have much time or energy left for Anthony, who can take good care of himself, thank you very much, but who gets sad when he realizes how unimportant he seems to be. Who would you choose, the warm and embracing family or the one that doesn't welcome you? Who would you be more generous to, the niece and nephew you are connected with or the ones you barely know at all? Where would you prefer to spend time?

I tell this story because the contrast between the two families is so stark. I'm sure that Anthony's in-laws aren't perfect, but he doesn't notice. And his sister and her husband may have a few things to say about the judgmental brother and his wife who probably exchange knowing looks when they visit. But if you want a brother or sister back, you might start by treating the couple the way you treat dear friends. It doesn't always work, but one of the things that keep siblings together is persistence, which is a great virtue in families.

Somewhere between the brothers and sisters who overcome centrifugal force and those who have found that small conflicts become big ones are the brothers and sisters who bobble between close and distant, trying to adjust to the situation as it changes. I think of two brothers who were fine together, but not that close, until they married women who love each other and brought the couples together. Or a family so embracing that even the ex-wives come to family celebrations and are made welcome. So often it comes down to having a unique relationship with the in-law, not one that is guided by the spouse. The days of telephone landlines made this easier, because you never knew who would pick up the phone at the house. You might get a chance for a short chat with the in-law. Now when everybody speaks on their own cell phones, those fruitful chance encounters aren't so common. But small gestures of acceptance and kindness have away of breaking down barriers over time.

A TALE OF TWO BROTHERS

Keith used to cook with his older brother, and his sister-in-law refused to touch their creations. The backstory is iconic: their mother and the girlfriend fought early in their relationship, and never made up. The girlfriend took a strong dislike to the entire family. The brothers were driven to communicating by e-mail. The brothers had been close as kids, sharing interests and dealing together with their parents, but they could not bridge the gap the eldest brother's marriage created. Years of coldness and distance ended only when this couple divorced. These two had always been much closer than Keith and his younger brother, who is eight years his junior and very different from the cultured, artistic Keith. The younger brother is into cars and beer, pranks and terrible music. Keith sees him as an overgrown adolescent. "He's in the mechanical world, where they talk about sports and what things cost and drink cheap beer. He goes to concerts because it's a band he liked in high school." They didn't have much in common for most of their lives; it felt as if they came from different worlds.

When this brother was in his twenties, he married a woman with three children; she'd had them all by the time she was nineteen. But strangely, in this strict Catholic family, she has brought the brothers together. She's energetic and warm, and even Keith's judgmental parents can't resist her. So what if she made some bad decisions as a teenager, they reasoned; she brought them three new grandkids. Keith loves having these children around, and he has become his younger brother's coach, helping him be a better husband and father.

The wife is attending nursing school at night, and Keith's brother needs to shoulder some of the child care. Keith has taken it upon himself to help his little brother see the world through his wife's (bleary) eyes. What a difference. When his younger brother finds himself in trouble, Keith helps out, usually by siding with the wife and pointing out her side of it. "And now he will send me silly e-mails or dumb forwards that I don't need to see," Keith says, "but I'll open them anyway. I'm not ever going to tell him to stop."

Keith's two brothers are a contrast in ease and intimacy. Nobody could overcome the opening moments of his older brother's marriage. Keith is lucky that his younger brother came to the game after his older brother and their parents had learned their lesson. He didn't have to fight his way out of the middle.

Christina comes from a very different kind of family. They fight and have it out, they talk it out, and they love one another to pieces. Christina, who tells me she doesn't know how to keep her mouth shut, is very close to her younger brother. She mothered him when he was a child, and they used to vacation together before he got married. She cannot imagine life without him.

CHRISTINA STIRS THE POT

Christina comes from a robust Italian family where food and talk and laughter fill the room. Her family style helps explain why Christina took it upon herself to let her brother know he was losing them. Christina says that if a baby was born on a Thursday, "by Sunday the baby was sitting in the infant seat on the table next to the bowl of macaroni. He was passed from place to place. If a meatball fell on him, that's fine." But when her little brother married a girl who came from a different culture, things got tense. She's a nice woman, but she is the kind of person who counts the dinner rolls—that's not the style of Christina's family. When they came to visit with their first child, it was awful. Christina shakes her head. "Rules kicked into place. You couldn't look at the baby, you're overstimulating her." It got worse: "When they'd come to visit, they'd take her right upstairs and put her in a bedroom, and put on a baby monitor, and we would sit in the living room listening to the monitor." Christmas Eve, which was always a source of joy to the family, became a nightmare because her brother and his wife insisted on keeping to their normal schedule, bathing the baby during the long dinner and taking her home to sleep in her own bed before the presents were opened. Christina and her sisters blamed the wife for imposing this new order on the family and for distancing her husband from them.

Then one day Christina's brother dropped by her office. He needed her advice. He was thinking of taking a job in another city, near his wife's family. "What do you think?" he asked. "Should I move away from the family? I really want Mom and Dad to be a part of the kids' lives, and if I move away, they're going to become the grandparents they see a few times a year." Christina grins and continues, "I, being the one who stirs the pot, said, 'Well, it's not like they see you that much anyway.'" She saw the shock on his face and plunged right in. "You're not really plugged into their lives. They're not really plugged into yours, because you have all these rules, and when you come over to visit, we can't look at the kids." Her brother was flabbergasted. "He was more shocked than furious," she says. "When he told his wife, she was hysterical." I wasn't surprised to hear that, but the rest was an eye-opener: "She was so upset that we thought she didn't want to be close, and she was remorseful. She felt she had been misunderstood." Christina visited with her brother and his wife to continue the conversation: "She cried, I cried, he cried, everybody cried. But it was something that needed to be said." And from then on, they made a genuine effort. "And you know what?" Christina says. "Once you make the effort, then it doesn't feel like an effort. It becomes more natural."

Christina had enough confidence in the strength of their relationship to speak up and clear the air. But she does not come by her fearlessness by accident. This is a matter of family style: the sisters and their brother spent all their lives arguing, making up, hurting each other's feelings, and forgiving each other. Christina's oldest sister was cruel to her. She told Christina that she was adopted. Cleverly, she warned Christina that her parents would always deny that truth—they wanted to keep the secret. So when Christina confronted her parents, they denied the story—but that is what her sister had warned her would happen, so she still believed she was adopted. This mean older sister also told Christina that the photographer who came once a year to take a family picture was planning to take Christina away with him after the photo shoot. That explains the look of terror on Christina's face in these family portraits, but nothing can explain the closeness of those sisters now. Except, perhaps, for the many times when she apologized and Christina eventually forgave her. They never stopped talking.

Robin's littlest brother died when he was only six (she was eight years old), and the tragedy silenced the family. Her older brothers became taciturn, and it took their wives to open them up to Robin.

ROBIN'S JOY

"I really hope you guys never split up because I'm going to have custody of you. I'll have visitation with my brother, but I want custody of you."
—Robin to her sister-in-law

That's how Robin feels about her oldest brother's wife. "My sister-in-law's so gregarious and we have a ball together," she says. When Robin goes home from his house, her brother will say, "Man, I didn't get to spend much time with Robin." Robin thinks, "But he didn't say anything when we were together!" At least she knows he cares.

Robin's older brothers shut down after the death of their little brother. From the funeral on, Robin tells me, those boys didn't communicate with her, except to express criticism. The brothers beat up on Robin all her life, especially for being overweight. She thought her brothers hated her. It wasn't until her older brother married that Robin heard a kind word from him. Naturally, she adores his wife: "She's effervescent. And we're very much alike. We're both very gregarious and we just love to laugh, probably to the point of annoyance for both my husband and my brother." I hear the joy in Robin's voice when she talks about her sister-in-law. She visits her older brother's family at least twice a year, and they have a ball. "One day, we found ourselves sitting at a roadside little burger/ice cream joint. There had to be a hundred and fifty people just sitting around, having ice cream." Robin said, "I don't have this where I live, and I miss this." Her sister-in-law looked around and replied, "We're just sitting here eating ice cream and loving life." That comment has become Robin's mantra. She says, "And that's what we do together. We just eat ice cream and love life."

Robin's next brother recently married an excellent woman. Robin describes her as "one of the most nonjudgmental people I've ever known." This means a lot to Robin, who is especially tender in the department of judgment. If she had to rank them, the original sister-in-law would take first place, but the second one has been generous to Robin's little brother.

He recently became ill, lost his mobility and his job, and slipped into depression and debt. Robin's middle brother, prompted by his wife, came to the rescue. They helped him out financially, putting him on an allowance until he got out of debt. Now he is on disability and has become an ace at economizing.

This sister-in-law does her financial planning with her husband's brother in mind. Robin is in awe. "If they buy a piece of land, they're going to buy something big enough to put a place on it for our brother. Because they're always going to be looking out for him and responsible for him." And this isn't her blood. This is her husband's brother.

Much of this is beyond our control. Some people just like each other, and others feel like permanent strangers. It comes down to affinity, that indescribable sense of familiarity and comfort. People like Robin and Keith have natural affinities with the wives of their brothers. But it just might be possible for cooler brothers- and sisters-in-law to find moments of ease, patches of similarity, shared views—if they look for them. It might even be possible to fly the white flag from time to time. If we can build a small area of shared feelings, we can always grow it. Families where the anger and hurt are old and deep may think that there is not much to be done, and they may be right. But for others, for those lucky enough to share ambivalence instead of dislike, signaling the desire for peace, admitting some culpability for the tensions, and expressing genuine appreciation for what you think is okay might just be of some help. If it doesn't improve the situation, at least you'll know you did your best.

The earlier this begins, the better. In fact, I think we should add another vow to the wedding ceremony: that bride and groom and brothers and sisters promise to stay connected and communicating, accepting one another's weirdness and always looking for ways to express their love for one another. Call it the Affinity Clause. I'm ready to add it. What about you?

6

WHEN DIFFERENCE
LEADS TO DISTANCE

Imagine a cartoon with two people who look alike sitting across the table from each other, thinking. The balloon above one of them says, "Why can't you be just like me?" The balloon above the other character says, "Why can't you just let me be?" This is an eternal complaint of grown brothers and sisters whose lives have diverged, whose interests have taken them to different places, or who have genuine disagreements about values.

It bothers us a lot more than we think it should—and probably more than it ought to, in a perfect world. Politics, religion, and money are always hot-button subjects, but between brothers and sisters they can be explosive. We are in a triple bind: we blame ourselves for not being able to influence their choices; we blame them for their behavior; and we blame ourselves for letting it bother us so much. So our thoughts go round in circles:

What difference does it make if we don't agree about
   politics or religion—we're still family, aren't we?
How can we come from the same family when we see the
   world so differently?
Why do I let it get under my skin?

When we find ourselves insulted by their choices or when
their behavior hurts our feelings or our pride, we respond in
anger, or we withdraw. Brothers and sisters find it extremely difficult to agree to disagree.

The problem is the powerful push and pull that lies beneath
the surface. Our shared childhoods create a strong attachment,
even while the ways in which we have differentiated ourselves
draw us apart. The merging of brothers and sisters who shared
almost everything and wanted to be alike is still at war with the
imperative to differentiate. Imagine a jigsaw puzzle. A brother
has this piece; a sister has another one. Some pieces are so similar in color and shape that they look like duplicates (that's
what we share), but many of them are different (that's what
makes us individuals). I met a woman whose father was the
high school music teacher in their town. All his children played
a musical instrument—and they'd each chosen a different one.
They were not trying to create an orchestra; that's just what
kids do. This is one of the many sibling paradoxes: we distin-
guish ourselves from our siblings, but after a lifetime of doing
that, the distance between us increases. A small act or choice
can touch a nerve, and we jump.

It takes energy to stay annoyed at a sibling's wastefulness, say,
or lack of social graces, or politics. That energy comes from the
nursery; it fuels our irritation and at the same time makes it
hard to let our siblings go. I am talking about legitimate differ-

ences that infuriate brothers and sisters. We face a dilemma, giving up on them or easing up on them, so we throw up our hands.

Lori and her two older sisters had alcoholic parents who would stay out all night and wake the girls up with their loud talk and rowdy laughter in the early hours of the morning. The oldest sister disappeared into her own world, what Lori calls "her bubble," and got out of the house as soon as she could. Her middle sister's departure three years later left Lori to raise herself, cook and clean for herself, and keep the secret of her hard life from the world. She sees herself as an only child with two sisters, and that informs her mixed feelings about them. Her cold and lonely childhood left scars on Lori, and it created the foundation for the conflict with her middle sister.

MICAH'S PLACE

On a beautiful October morning, Lori welcomes me into her home. Her porch is covered in plants of all sizes and shapes. Her living room is full of small objects—china figurines, pretty glassware, and photographs of family and friends. The candles on her fireplace mantel are lit and shed a soft light through the room.

Lori has pretty much given up on her oldest sister, who has insulated herself from conflict and intimacy. It's the next sister, the middle one, who gets under Lori's skin. They used to be close. When Lori was first married and raising her four kids, her sister lived nearby. Lori's kids adored their "most favorite auntie," and Lori felt the same about her sister. Over the course of those years, Lori found it harder and harder to leave the house, finally descending into agoraphobia. Lori thinks she couldn't have survived without her faith and her belief in a personal savior; her married sister, Anna, was also a great help.

When Anna found herself pregnant with another man's child, she decided to hide the affair from her husband by having an abortion; she thought it would save her marriage. Lori, who opposes abortion on moral grounds, held her tongue during this period and was relieved when her sister, whose marriage did not survive, remarried. But as Lori watched Anna suffer miscarriage after miscarriage around the anniversary of the abortion, her hatred of the procedure deepened. It was a relief when her sister was able to carry a baby until the time for amnio, but then they discovered that the baby had Down syndrome. Anna decided on another abortion. Lori was beside herself. After the procedure was over, the doctors realized that they had miscalculated the extent of the pregnancy and that the fetus was close enough to viability to require a birth certificate. Lori's heart broke for her sister, and she was in a white rage over the whole situation and the death of the baby, whom Anna named Micah.

Lori was by then living in a small town where her husband had been transferred, and she still could not leave the house. Then she got the idea to start a clinic to inform pregnant women about the physical, emotional, and moral evils of abortion. Her fierce passion on the subject opened the doors in Lori's life. She overcame the agoraphobia, and now she travels around the country on her mission to oppose abortion. Lori called the first waiting room Micah's Place.

This is a source of great pain for both women. Anna sees her sister's activities as a rebuke, especially Lori's decision to name the waiting room after Micah. Lori sees it as honoring the tragedy and making sure it doesn't happen again. Lori is an evangelical Christian and a conservative Republican. Anna is an atheist Democrat. When they were young, survival was their goal. Religion and politics didn't matter. But their lives diverged, their beliefs hardened, and now they can barely stand to be together in the same room.

As Lori says, "Our differences manifest into political differences, spiritual differences, cultural, everything, so they are just magnified." After their father died, she recalls, "The first night, we're sitting on our front porch, and we're just talking, and my sister starts on about the war in Iraq. I thought, Oh, great, here we go, right off the bat." What's so interesting about this is that Anna is as angry as Lori; she started this particular fight. Lori says that the discussion about the war didn't take an hour before "she was storming out of here, and she said she was going to leave the next morning." Disagreements over war and politics are good exit permits.

I asked Lori where the oldest sister stands. "Blissfully neutral," she answered. "She's in her bubble. You're not going to get controversy when you talk to her." It's a smart strategy to stay out of the fray. Even though your connections are tenuous, it keeps you out of trouble. Lori blames herself for this particular fight. "I'm the rabble-rouser. I disturbed their life from the get-go." They're both at fault. Anna can't control herself from raising these hot-button subjects; Lori cannot keep herself from responding in kind. They need each other, but they can't stand each other. Their bonds cannot be broken, so they torture each other.

Recently Lori's oldest child got married. She invited both sisters but expected neither to come. Lori grins. "We were at the rehearsal dinner, and all of a sudden, I am thinking, Where did everybody go? They're all missing." Her husband said, "Oh, didn't you know? Anna's here." Lori smiled and said, "No way." She went outside to check. "I'm just standing in the parking area going, I can't believe she drove by herself from Texas." She was thrilled, and when Anna left the wedding the next day without saying good-bye, Lori phoned the hotel and told her how much she appreciated her coming for the wedding: "That meant a lot to me, and to my son and all my kids." Her sister continued the good feeling: "Well, it was just wonderful. It was a beautiful wedding. I'm glad I came." Then came the comment that sums up their relationship: "I didn't take any of the silver," Anna said. Lori shakes her head. "When you get a little too close, she puts up her wall."

I think the fact that they keep on sparring is a sign of how much they mean to each other. Some day they may recognize that fact and give themselves a little respite from their battles. If not, weddings will suffice. No silver will be taken, and no hearts broken.

Plenty of brothers and sisters content themselves with being Wedding and Wake siblings. They're not close, and they rub each other the wrong way, but they recognize the importance of family, even if they don't particularly enjoy each other's company. This is a good solution for many people who find it a relief no longer to feel that they ought to love each other and look forward to being together, but who do not want to be enemies. For some people, family occasions are like the Sabbath Truce, a military tradition that grew up in Europe—troops ceased fighting on Sundays, and they might even meet and share a meal or a smoke. The next day they would get back to the business of trying to kill each other. Brothers and sisters who don't get along often declare a truce at important family times. But you never know when the war will erupt again, and life's twists and turns can increase the hostilities.

Money is often one of those divisive elements. Whenever there are discrepancies or changes of fortune among siblings, we revert to childhood. The old competitions, the old jealousies, the roles we took as kids return with a fury, and it is hard to tell adult responses from the childish ones. When the lifestyle of a brother or sister dramatically changes for the better, the nonrich siblings feel as if their values have been betrayed. There may be envy when brothers and sisters judge the wealthy one's behavior: "She's so materialistic"; "What do they need such a big house for?" "Not my values," they think, which may be true, but there's no way of telling what anybody would do under such circumstances. If the wealthy sibling is thinking, "Whose business is it how I spend my money?" that makes sense, too.

A couple of years ago, during the economic boom, I spoke to a group of men and women who had made their fortunes at a relatively early age. My topic was how parents and their grown children deal with one another, but they wanted to talk about what their wealth had done to their relationships with their siblings. It was not a happy conversation; they felt guilty about the differences in lifestyle; they didn't understand why their generosity—or its opposite—had caused such trouble among their siblings. They were surprised that their wealth was making such waves in the family.

I think this may be the plight of Donna's wealthy sister, because she is the object of such fury. Competition that began in the nursery has taken on a new and painful dimension.

REVERSAL OF FORTUNE

The sisters grew up in a comfortable home, just two years apart in age. The smart one came first, followed by Donna, the pretty one. The smart one was always jealous of her younger sister's successes, in school and socially. Donna resented being typed as pretty—she is smart, too, after all. When Donna married and had children, they lived in the same neighborhood. Donna was happy to share her children with her older sister, and she basked in her role as wife and mother. Reversals of fortune are the law, not the exception, as we all know. Everybody was upset when Donna's husband asked for a divorce and Donna's marriage and security vanished. It was humiliating, but she soldiered on, supplementing her alimony payments with her mother's help.

Donna's socially inept older sister did eventually get married, but to an unimpressive guy who toiled in the IT department of a local business. This match was not a cause for celebration in the family, although everybody was relieved that her sister had landed a husband. He worked in the back room, dealing with inventory and such. Over time, he invented an excellent database. With her brains and his invention, they started a company that became successful. Now the smart sister was also the rich sister. She showed her love for Donna by arranging to get her a job in the business. Donna was delighted. "I started doing really, really well in the organization, and making nice money, and feeling really good about myself. It was a terrific thing for me to have that independence."

Then her sister got pregnant and stopped working. Donna was happy for her and especially pleased because now she could talk with her brother-in-law about the business at family gatherings. She enjoyed these conversations, Donna tells me. "All of a sudden I became the smart one." Donna was not smart about one thing: the competition that still existed between the sisters. "You could see her getting more and more furious," she says. "She was always mad at me for being pretty. Always." Now she was mad at Donna for being smart. This was not a good situation.

Donna's sister—who remained on the board of the company even though she no longer worked there—arranged for her to be promoted to a job with a better title but a vague set of responsibilities. Donna began to struggle in her job. When her brother-in-law brought in an old friend to help him put the business up as an IPO, the new executive didn't appreciate Donna, so they decided to transfer her to a less responsible position, at the same salary. A novice in business, she quit in a rage instead of holding on until the company went public. Donna feels betrayed, blames her sister, and will never forgive her. Donna's sister can't understand this—after all, they didn't fire her, they just changed her job; and they did what was best for the business.

Donna thinks her sister's mansion is in bad taste. She resents the fact that her sister can entertain the whole family at her enormous table, without going to any effort (Donna resents her sister's staff, too). She derides their philanthropy—to Donna it looks like a brazen attempt at upward mobility, not true generosity. When it comes to her own daughters, Donna believes her sister is trying to buy their affection when she invites them to lunch or to some interesting event. They have always loved their aunt and are mystified when their mother considers them traitors for continuing to accept her invitations and enjoy her company. Family gatherings, which her sister insists on hosting, are torture. Donna can barely exchange words with her sister and brother-in-law, and moves from room to room to avoid them in their own home. Donna dreams of severing all ties with her sister, but she can't. It would set a poor example for her daughters, whom she wants to be close; and, of course, for all the pain and rage, Donna's sister is still her sister.

Donna won all the competitions of their childhood. Then her sister moved into the lead. Her sister compounded the problem by both hiring Donna and then demoting her. Donna knew when she was making her sister jealous, and she takes no responsibility for that. She cannot see any of her sister's actions as generous or loving.

Donna's sister's side of the story might run like this: She didn't fire her sister; she just transferred her—to keep her from being let go. It was Donna who quit. She isn't trying to steal her nieces; she is being generous. She isn't hosting the big family dinners to hurt Donna's feelings; her house is big enough to hold them all. In fact, she loves her sister and wishes they weren't at war. I can tell from Donna's stories that her sister wants to be forgiven and the hostilities to cease. The problem is that the competition between them was set up long before anybody had a fortune, and it is extremely hard to shed the feelings that were nourished in the nursery.

It doesn't have to be that way. Recently I was speaking with a woman whose brother became extremely wealthy, thanks to an invention of his. It came as a surprise to his sisters, but they were happy for him. When he endowed a concert hall, this woman's nose wasn't put out of joint; she thought it was a great thing to do. Even when he quietly set up a trust fund for her daughter's education, she didn't think he was trying to steal her; she thought her brother was being generous. I asked her if she was jealous. "No," she said, "it's his life. We're happy for him." When their little sister was down on her luck after a difficult divorce, their brother called this woman and asked, "Do you think it would be okay if I bought her an apartment in a better neighborhood with better schools for the kids?" She thought about it and said, "If you wouldn't notice the difference without this money, then do it." He bought the younger sister the apartment. The other sister says, "What a nice thing he did."

One of the reasons why these siblings are not torn apart by their disparate wealth, I think, is because as kids, they banded together to take care of one another when the parents were not available to them. That bond of mutual protection is supple and strong. The sisters have no sense of entitlement to their brother's wealth. Their positive attitude is more a result of the past than of the present.

Small differences can also irk siblings, as we all know. One successful professional I know raised her children while holding down a demanding job. For many years, she was rankled by the fact that her sister spent all her time shopping, and never worked at all. She used to joke that her sister knew the stock of all Chicago's Magnificent Mile stores like the back of her hand. The sisters kept up a relationship, mind you, but the disparities in their lives led to constant complaints. Then at some point the complaints stopped. I asked her what had happened. "We got older," she said, "and we've all had troubles. It just doesn't matter to me anymore." That perspective isn't resignation,

I think—it's more like the acceptance we may offer others and hope someday to receive.

It didn't take Kelly most of her life to grow into this level of acceptance. She seems to have come by it naturally. The differences between her and her siblings never gave her pause.

KELLY DOES A VICTORY DANCE

I actually saw it. Kelly got up and danced a jig, barefoot in her sawed-off jeans and man's shirt. This week, Kelly tells me, she finally paid off her last credit card (it had gone as high as $38,000), which is how she financed college and law school (and helped her sister out). But now that she has joined a local law firm, she's finally out of debt, and she is hopping around the room with joy.

I was sitting on a couch in Kelly's new house on a warm autumn day. Cartons were stacked everywhere. I came to interview Kelly's boyfriend, but he was delayed at school—his parent-teacher meetings were running late—so Kelly took some time off from unpacking to talk to me. The cartons came from her old apartment. She and her boyfriend and another guy have just bought this house, and they are thrilled. I can see why. It's a roomy place, with good, odd spaces and lots of light. October sunlight pours in from the deck outside the living room. As I glance out the window, I can picture endless cookouts and parties and good times. Kelly is a lanky and loose-jointed redhead with hazel eyes that twinkle. She speaks with the cadences of an educated woman, but when she talks about her childhood, she falls into a country accent.

Kelly, the youngest of three, was always the responsible one. She and her brother are extremely close in age (a little over a year apart) and were best friends throughout their childhood. They lived on a farm miles away from a tiny town, and they were like two baby cubs, playing outside, climbing trees, and torturing their older sister. You don't want to know what Kelly and her brother did to their older sister's dolls. The family lived so far from the school that Kelly and her brother rode the bus an hour and a half each way together, five days a week. They didn't talk much at school, but they loved those rides. Neither of them was close to the older sister.

By the time they were teenagers, the ordinary tensions had arisen. Kelly recalls, "Everybody had a three-wheeler or four-wheeler or a motorcycle, and we were fighting to see who was going to go driving. We were never that close after that." Their paths began to diverge when her brother opted for the vocational training track in high school; Kelly was outstanding academically. Then, when he was a senior, he fell in love with an eighth grader, and they got married pretty young. Kelly didn't approve. "I mean, her parents were okay with it, my parents weren't, but [she shrugs] they're still married." Her brother became an expert craftsman, and customers travel hundreds of miles to hire him, but brother and sister have not found it easy to reconnect. Even though they live an hour's drive apart, Kelly's brother never comes to visit.

What surprised me is how close Kelly and her older sister have become. She married young and is now a single mom, supporting two kids with minimal help from her former husband. She's good with numbers, Kelly tells me, and she worked for years as a bookkeeper. That would have been fine if she hadn't decided to pad her paycheck by embezzling small amounts of money from the business. She almost got away with it, until the IRS did an audit. When she got caught, her parents bailed her out and repaid the stolen money. Now, that might be enough to break up these two sisters who were never close, don't you think? After all, Kelly chose a career in law. But somehow the sympathy between them has grown over time. Kelly has helped her sister out more often than she likes to think. "Financially she's a mess," Kelly says. "In the midst of paying off my own credit card debt, I'd hate to think how much money I've given her. She has her own subcategory in my Quicken book, which I don't click on anymore—it just depresses me to realize how much money I've fronted to my sister and her kids." At least now her sister has a good job and is getting to the point where she can support herself and her children. Kelly has figured out a way to help her sister but keep control: "If she wants me to pay her utility bill once a winter, I'll make the check out to them." Smart.

So here is Kelly, the youngest who was always the most responsible (when her parents went away for a weekend, leaving their twelve-year-old daughter in charge, they secretly gave Kelly, the seven-year-old, an emergency stash of money). She and her brother were pals when they were kids, and now Kelly is much closer to her sister, the embezzler. Maybe her brother felt bad about not going the academic route and thought that Kelly shared their parents' disapproval of his marriage. He has also been very hard on their older sister, and he may resent the money their parents shelled out to repay her theft. A man who pays his own bills and earns his money with his own hands, Kelly's brother is busy with his work and his family, but Kelly doesn't think that is an excuse for the distance he keeps.

A month or so ago, the three were at their parents' home, and her sister commented to Kelly, "You know, when Mom and

Dad die, the three of us will never get together." Kelly said, "What the hell? Why would you say that?" Her sister said, "Well, you know he would never come around." Their brother was in another room, but he overheard her sister continue, "Me and you will still do stuff, but you know, hell, that's going to be it." A couple of weeks later, he called and took his older sister and all the kids to a St. Louis Cardinals ball game—and they had third-row seats. "Oh my gosh," Kelly says, "you would have thought that he just gave her the world. I mean, that little thing, just the fact that he shared tickets that he got for free with my sister and her kids, oh, she was floored." Later that summer, they all went on a picnic where there was swimming and fishing. There's a pause and then Kelly continues, "My sister thinks that my brother's finally growing up. I think both of them are growing up."

Kelly, the youngest, has waited for them to grow up. For the years between high school and now, these three siblings have taken widely different paths, but now they are coming together just a bit. Thinking about that sunny deck at Kelly's house, I picture another kind of gathering, when the sisters and their brother and their families get together for cookouts and silliness.

I wish I had a theory about how to overcome the differences that madden us and separate us from our brothers and sisters. I have a friend who uses this technique: put the shoe on the other foot. If you're outraged that a brother or sister is challenging your fundamental beliefs, put the shoe on the other foot and imagine how he or she might feel about the choices you have made. If your home is neat and your sister is a slob, imagine what she is thinking (while clucking secretly) about your immaculate kitchen. Once a friend came to visit me when my kids were small, and she greeted my alphabetized spices with a look of remonstrance—and she isn't even my sister. Do you find your brother an embarrassment when he insists on engaging with every cab driver and waitress in town? Maybe he thinks you're too cool for comfort.

Think about politics for a minute. Sure, it's fine to decide that you don't want to spend any more time with your lefty sister—but remember, she's put up with you all these years, too. And so it goes along the paths of divergence. What makes us so sensitive and allergic to these differences is in part the objective fact that we are right and they are wrong; but it's also a matter of that old childhood connection coming to the surface. Whenever we have overwhelming feelings about our brothers and sisters, a component of that power comes from the nursery, when we were supposed to be alike (or we believed that we should share everything). Growing up is about diverging; maturity is about accepting. It's a difficult transition, and nobody says we must make it.

In a world filled with friends who would be more appropriate as siblings than our own blood kin, we can separate from brothers and sisters whose ideas and ways are not ours. But when trouble comes along, as it inevitably does, brothers and sisters who put aside their differences and work together have an easier time than the siblings who remain at odds.

7

THICK AND THIN

Vertical relationships—grandparents, parents, children, and grandchildren—tend to dominate our thinking about family. We understand the turning of generations: first our grandparents go, and then we know that we will someday have to bury our parents; we pray that our children will outlive us. But there is no natural succession with our brothers and sisters, and that may be why so many close siblings worry about it. The silence about siblings, from the nursery throughout our lives, is especially problematic when illness strikes a brother or sister, or when a sibling dies.

Brothers and sisters who have grown up with a disabled sibling have a heavy burden, and a special opportunity. If the family mix is right, then they participate in the care and loving of the ill brother or sister, and their joint activities not only expand their souls but also strengthen their bonds. There's nothing quite like the pleasure of knowing that brothers and sisters are there for the one in need—even if they slip from time to time. Those slips are important, reminding everybody that we're not paragons, that we're capable of being small and selfish—even when we want to be good. Being loved despite our serious failings feels good, and behaving well under difficult circumstances does, too. It confirms the best we all can be, and it makes us feel more secure about our own future. We may be surprised by acts of kindness or strength we never expected, and we may even find ourselves rising to an occasion.

Emily and her three older brothers were already a team when their littlest brother was diagnosed with a severe neurological disease. They were young when Timmy first showed symptoms, and as they have grown up and matured with him, they have witnessed his bravery along with his decline. The gentleness in Emily and her brothers cannot begin to compensate for this family's travails and their sorrow. But their kindness and concern never flag.

ON TIMMY'S TEAM

Patience and perspective, joined by an appreciation of heroism, often come to brothers and sisters with a disabled sibling. Emily exhibits all that, and a genuine sweetness of spirit. She came to talk to me through a college friend. They bonded in school because they are so close to their families. Emily is the only girl in a family of five children. She's thirty-two, and her three older brothers are thirty-three, thirty-four, and thirty-six. Her younger brother is twenty-eight. Their parents raised them in a relaxed and caring atmosphere. Surrounded by boys, Emily remembers playing all the time, building forts, making up games, playing basketball, and swimming with her brothers at the beach in the summer. They were a physical family, and all the kids were involved in sports. She was on many high school teams, and her parents rarely missed a game of hers—or anybody else's. The parents had high academic standards and set rules for their kids, but Emily's small-town childhood sounds idyllic.

This is especially important because Timmy, her younger brother, fell ill when he was a kid. He has a rare genetic disorder that interferes with his neurological and muscular functioning, and the disease has gradually debilitated him. At first he had trouble with coordination, which was surprising in this athletic family, and when he came down with a bad case of the flu, Emily says, "he didn't recover very well, and it really knocked him out. For a while he lost the ability to hold a ball." The general run of childhood illnesses hit Timmy especially hard; each siege depleted his physical capacity in some new way. This didn't stop Timmy. Instead of playing on varsity teams, he enjoyed pickup games—which the family attended with zeal no different from high school championship matches. He eventually needed a wheelchair, but he graduated from high school on time and began college. "Then four or five years ago he got really, really sick," Emily continues. He had convulsions and was in a coma for weeks. Timmy woke up without the brain damage everybody feared, but his physical situation had deteriorated. He could no longer get around by himself—even in the wheelchair—and he needed 24-7 attention. Today Timmy cannot be left alone, and he can't swallow anymore, so he has a feeding tube. The list of insults to Timmy's person grows. That doesn't stop Emily and her brothers from adoring him.

"Timmy is amazing," she says. "He's so upbeat. He works so hard. You see somebody go through physical therapy, or go through taking the amount of vitamins that he has to, and he doesn't complain."

Timmy has a deliciously sly sense of humor. "He can't speak as fast as other people, and so he just sits and sort of takes things in. But then he'll make some comment that is either hilarious or insightful, or really supportive. He's very, very funny," Emily says. Timmy has tutored neighborhood children and has shown a rare sense of empathy. "So he was trying to teach fractions," she tells me, "and I heard him start trying to explain it. Started talking about, you cut an apple into four pieces. That's one quarter. And she was listening to him and nodding, and I heard him talking about quarters as part of a dollar. And he said, 'Well, how many quarters in a dollar?' And she said, 'Four.' And then he said, 'How about a quarter of an hour?' And she said, 'There are four of those in an hour.' He just made these leaps, and I could hear her hook on to them."

This hasn't been easy, she tells me. "When I was a freshman in college, he was a freshman in high school. I would come home, and he would be swearing, he'd be staying up late. There were a lot less rules for him." Emily was frustrated, thinking it wasn't fair. Her mom took her aside one day. "I remember her telling me that he wasn't going to have friends the way I had friends, and he wasn't going to socialize the way I had," Emily says. Her mother explained that they decided that we would be different with him, because he would need that. Emily realized what a wise thing her mother was doing. "Of course, it still frustrated me sometimes, and I bitched about it, but I just thought that was incredible. I really respected that mentality of seeing what each kid needs, and acting a little bit differently."

As Timmy's health deteriorates, the burden on Emily's parents is severe. Insurance pays for a few hours of an aide each week, but that is far from enough. Their father now works at home and takes over for their mother during parts of the day. Here's where the team spirit comes in. Now that they are all grown up and live away from home, Emily and her older brothers rotate weekends to come home, so they can take turns helping out. They each choose one weekend a month. But they miss one another's company, so every once in a while they give themselves the treat of everybody coming home the same weekend. That way they can be together while helping out with Timmy.

Timmy doesn't give up and keeps doing whatever his body allows him to. He is his family's hero. He has taught Emily to slow down and listen. His perseverance has shown her what it means to keep on going even when you're tired or discouraged. Timmy has never lost his sense of humor and won't allow himself to get depressed.

The unspoken part of our conversation, the one that might worry you (it worries me), is what will happen to this family when the inevitable happens to Timmy. Here is everything I know: they have been a team for decades; they have all helped, so nobody is on the outs; they talk all the time, and they believe in communication as the foundation of their relationships. And they have learned from Timmy about courage, survival, and love. This family understands their profound interdependence. The fact that they have all been in this together should help sustain them.

It is a wholly different experience to be the only brother or sister who takes responsibility for the one in need. A lifetime spent caring for an ill sibling, without help from the others, can make you angry and increase your sense of isolation. Elizabeth grew up in a family full of dissension, and she was the butt of a lot of anger and teasing. That's because she was the rebel, she defied the family's ways, and she was her father's favorite. She never gave a thought to abandoning her older brother when he was in need; they were very close. Elizabeth's oldest brother and younger sister, on the other hand, were never there for either of them.

"HE'S MY FAMILIAR"

A woman who combines warmth and sophistication, Elizabeth grew up in a small town in the Midwest. Articulate and funny, she never misses a chance to laugh out loud. Now in her late fifties, she has helped her older brother through the decades of his mental illness and has survived her own brush with death. Her bond with George is built to last.

Elizabeth's family was visited by tragedy before she was born, and again when she was an infant. Her mother was widowed when her first son was a baby; that was the first tragedy. Three years later she married Elizabeth's father. Another son followed quickly, and then seventeen months later, a fussy baby girl, Elizabeth, arrived. One day when her mother was in the living room having a hard time feeding her and quieting her down, the doorbell rang. Her oldest brother was out playing with friends, and George was upstairs, asleep in his crib. Her mother opened the front door, and the next thing she knew a woman holding George in her arms was saying, "I think I have your toddler here." Her mother was so distracted with Elizabeth that she said, "Would you please put him on the couch while I finish feeding the baby?"

This was the second tragedy. George had crawled out of his crib, climbed up to the window, and fallen two stories to the sidewalk. His skull had a six-inch crack. In the hospital, George would say to his momma, "Hing, Mommy, hing," and she would sing to him endlessly. Elizabeth's mom was Catholic, and the priest to whom she went for comfort wouldn't say much more than "Well, the Lord giveth and the Lord taketh away." She promised that if George lived she would have a mass said in his honor, which she did, and then she left the church. She never went back. "His life was really saved because he was wearing his baseball cap," Elizabeth tells me.

Even though she was the youngest child in the family for the next nine years, Elizabeth became her older brother's caretaker. "George is the smartest of all of us. He was a straight A student," she says, and then her eyes fill with tears. "George and I, we did everything together when we were little. George is also a beautiful man, and he's so talented; he's such a good musician. I could show you little paintings he's painted. He's got every talent a person could want." The tears in her eyes come from the third tragedy. When he was in his twenties, George developed a serious mental illness and has been incapacitated on and off the rest of his life. When he is okay, the sister and brother talk and joke, reminisce and help each other. But when the bad times come, she can't even find him.

After college, Elizabeth moved to New York. She had a successful career on Wall Street and now heads a nonprofit organization. George followed her to the city when she was starting out. "He first came to New York when things really fell apart, and I actually got him on welfare," she tells me. In her twenties, Elizabeth was already the sole caretaker of her brother. "My dad wouldn't give him money if he was in New York," Elizabeth says, so she did what she could. "I used to have him for dinner at least once a week so I knew he'd had a good meal." George would be very depressed, and then he'd flip and get manic. When he became too crazy for her to deal with, Elizabeth sent him home. This is the report she got from her dad: "When we picked him up at the airport, he insisted on riding home in the trunk because he was afraid that his thoughts were going to come out and explode you, Elizabeth." Her mother wanted nothing to do with this son. Who knows what she suffered? Elizabeth's mother was a "life-of-the-party gal," but then she'd fall into what they called "Mom's bugged moods," where she would basically do nothing but sleep and play solitaire for months at a time. Elizabeth's older brother had left the house as soon as he could—he lived thousands of miles away—and her little sister was too young to be of any help.

Elizabeth's father recognized her superb head for business when she was a kid sitting on his lap and counting his pennies, which made her siblings jealous. She endured teasing and tearing down from all of them and became accustomed to their anger and irony. When things got really bad, she would respond, "You guys will come and laugh at my funeral." Noticing the look of shock on my face, Elizabeth adds, "I used to say that all the time."

She paid a heavy price for her brains and leadership when her father put George's share of his estate in trust and appointed Elizabeth the administrator. Her father's deathbed instruction—"Make it last as long as you can"—caused trouble. George wanted control of his patrimony and was furious with his sister. She resented this responsibility and felt terrible when he got angry. She says, "It was humiliating for him, and it made him furious. Why was I in charge of his money? Who was I to control him?" But she was resolute about following her father's wishes.

Then Elizabeth was diagnosed with stage 3 cancer. While Elizabeth was sick, she decided to be more forthcoming with her brother's money, since she thought she could be dead before she'd doled it all out. George immediately began to burn through the rest of his inheritance. Neither her brothers nor her sister came to see her when she was in the thick of the treatment. "I remember my friend saying, 'I can't believe you have cancer and your sister hasn't come here.'" Elizabeth shakes her head. They did show up eventually, but it was near the end of the treatment. "I somehow got the role of my father in the family," she explains. This is such a common and sad spot for siblings to find themselves in, taking on the persona of a parent, with all the responsibilities and few of the benefits.

By the time Elizabeth recovered—the chemotherapy worked—George had run through his inheritance. So she writes him a check every month. She doesn't mind. She considers it part of her living expenses, along with electricity and the mortgage on her home. "George has said to me many, many times, 'If it weren't for you, I wouldn't be here. There's no way I can thank you. It's not possible; you've done too much for me.'"

There's a postscript to Elizabeth's story. Elizabeth got fired when the nonprofit lost its endowment in the financial crisis of 2008. Because she could no longer afford to give George as much money as before, she turned to her other brother and sister for help. She was amazed: they pitched in, to the extent they could. They still cannot contribute as much as Elizabeth, but they are helping support their brother, and they are helping their sister, who shouldered this burden alone for so many years. Her reversal of fortune has made her feel a little less alone.

Elizabeth watched my reaction as I listened to her stories, and she wanted me to understand that her childhood was not all bad. "There was an intact family and there were family vacations. I'm telling you the bad stuff because that always seems to last longer than the good stuff. I don't know—why does pain last so much longer than pleasure? I don't know why, but it does."

Pain does outlast pleasure. We are hardwired to be more responsive to danger than to delight, and pain is danger's messenger. Elizabeth believed she had to care for George as soon as she was old enough to understand what happened that terrible morning when she was a fussy baby. But the burden of guilt for George's accident doesn't explain why she has been such a faithful caretaker, and why she is doing her best to mend things with her other siblings. How she dealt with her brother's troubles, and her lifelong dedication to him have expanded her soul. She is a survivor in every way. I think her strength was honed by her years as the outsider sister. But the part of her that cared for George also helped her navigate the difficulties in her own life. That is one of George's gifts to Elizabeth. The other is her other siblings' willingness to help.

But what if Elizabeth had died? Were the siblings close enough to help each other through such a tragedy? Happily, we'll never know, but we do know that the death of a brother or sister is a terrible shock to our notions of succession, and we end up both bereft and silent. How could it be that more books are available advising people about how to deal with the death of a pet than the death of a brother or sister? Professor T. J. Wray calls this "disenfranchised loss," and I think she is right.

If people lack the language to comfort a friend who has lost a brother or sister, the bereaved person feels even more alone. Silence in the face of these tragedies takes many forms: it can be seen in the lack of words of comfort, and in friends' inability to spend time listening to childhood stories and the recounting of the death. And if there is a surviving parent, that person is the mourner in chief, because losing a child is properly thought to be a greater tragedy. In these circumstances, the emotional availability of brothers and sisters is crucial. The death of a family member always puts a strain on everybody, because in moments of stress, we revert to our childish selves, and those primitive relationships push to the surface. For instance, there's usually a member of the family whom everybody gets mad at, before or after the funeral. My friend calls that person the "family goat." A mistake, a misstatement, somebody loses it, and all hell breaks loose. Or we are covered in guilt, not so much for the present situation but for all the past moments when we weren't good enough. Or we are angry in retrospect at the actions that were committed long before tragedy struck. In these moments, the quality of our closeness, the ability to talk without hurting each other, and the family style in dealing with hardship can make a difference. Brothers and sisters who lack support or aren't given the opportunity to offer it feel even more alone. This increases the burden. I don't mean these stories to be morality tales, but they carry a warning. In times of trouble, brothers and sisters may be all we have.

Tony comes from a family of five children, and, like Elizabeth, he wasn't close to his siblings. Tony thought he could go it alone. But he is grateful that he reconnected with his oldest brother.

THE LESSON

Looking at Tony today, you wouldn't know that he was born three months premature, weighing under two pounds. A gym teacher in a large public school, Tony is tall and muscular, with a bounce to his step and the energy to bring a group of slothful seventh graders to attention.

He looks tough, with his shoulder-length dreadlocks, and he commands respect, with his booming voice. Behind the facade is a thoughtful man who has dealt with his own pain. He had a hard childhood. When he was five, his mother sent all her kids from Philadelphia to visit their grandmother in Trinidad. Some of the children returned to the States, but Tony's visit lasted five years. By the time he came home, Tony had decided that he certainly didn't need his absent father, and that he could not depend on his brothers and sisters, either. He got himself an education and a career without anybody's help, and he basks in the approval and attention he gets from his students and peers.

The middle child, Tony has always been a leader. His can-do attitude and his bossiness are hallmarks of his relations with all his siblings. He loves taking charge, and that explains his success as a teacher—he has a way of telling you what to do with a big smile that you can't resist. The sense of isolation that often accompanies the role of family leader had made Tony feel abandoned—first by his father and then by his mother. The weight of his anger and sorrow finally got Tony down, and he was determined to heal himself. In his search for help, he enrolled in a behavior-modification program. The instructors convinced him that he couldn't duck his negative feelings any longer—if he did, the sadness and isolation would never abate. They urged him to resolve his issues with his father, whose behavior Tony could never accept. He says, "I thought, My father left me, he did not want me, so I don't need him; I can do this all on my own." The instructors insisted, "Go speak to your father." Tony understood their strategy. "The way they wanted you to speak to him was unbearable: not blame him for anything, not put him at fault, don't have him become defensive." By the end of the course, Tony's defenses were down. He agreed to talk to him. When he dialed his father's number, nobody picked up. His father doesn't have an answering machine. Tony went back to the group and said, "See? Even now when I need him, he didn't pick up the phone." "Well, speak to somebody else," the instructors said. The person who reminded him the most of his dad was his elder brother, Kevin, so he dialed his number. Tony relates their conversation: " 'Hi, it's me, Tony.' Kevin's like, 'Oh, you want to speak to Brian?' 'No, I wanted to speak to you.' "

Tony spoke to his brother the words that he was planning to say to their father: "So I am on the phone and I'm telling him that I really need him in my life, I need to have him a part of my life." His brother was astonished: "I would never expect this from you." For the first time, Tony recognized the part he'd played in his own isolation; he had always told himself, "I don't need your help. I can do this on my own."

For this moment, Tony stopped giving orders and started listening. "I got it that my brother loved me. So I am on the phone, in tears, listening to him talk. He's like, 'Are you okay? Are you all right?' I'm like, 'My brother loves me.' " It was a great relief. "I had this wonderful conversation with him." Tony says, "I'm the teacher, and he's telling me how to take care of myself. I thought, Wow, he wants the best for me."

Tony was in the teachers' lounge the following Friday when the school secretary stopped by and told him, "Stay by the phone. Your brother needs to speak to you." Tony said he had to run to his next class, but she insisted, "Stay here, please." Then his cell phone rang. His middle brother spoke: "I don't know how to tell you this." "Go ahead and tell me." "The house burned down. The house is gone, in flames." "Is everybody okay?" "Well, I don't know how to tell you this, but Kevin fell out the window."

Tony rushed to the hospital: "It was the longest train ride I ever took in my life. You're thinking something might happen to your brother, then you think to yourself, 'I'll make a bargain with You right now. I'll start going back to church again.' " When he arrived, Tony took the lead with the doctor: "You can tell me. Tell me now. I don't want to wait." The doctor couldn't look at him when he said, "Your brother did not make it." Tony wanted to scream, but he needed to protect his middle brother and speak to their mother. "So now I have to walk past the room, look at him, and make a phone call to my mom," he says. Tony gave his brother the Hawaiian surfers' hang loose sign, but "I couldn't face him, so I had to turn away." His mother already knew. They had pronounced Kevin dead at the scene. Then he turned to his brother. "I couldn't say the words. I started crying. From that, he knew." Tony had to mouth the words "Our brother passed away."

Tony, the only family member whose ID wasn't burned in the fire, went to the morgue to identify his brother. "It was a good thing they didn't have to pull out a slab. If they had done that, I probably would have lost it. They take Polaroid pictures of the person. The lady pulls out the envelope and she's looking at the picture and says, 'It looks just like you.' In the back of my mind, I'm like, 'Oh, man. That's my brother in there.'" Tony's voice gets very quiet as he tells me this story. We share a minute of silence.

And then, being the man he is, Tony finds a little uplift. "I remember they said whatever you are afraid of, the emotion that you're trying to push away, it's going to come back. They tell you to go back to that place and stay there for a bit—see what happens." He says, "I'm driving and I'm thinking about that picture, because I wanted to push that picture away. I'm looking at the picture in my mind and I'm starting to calm down. He looked like he was sleeping. He looked like he was peaceful."

Tony, his mother, and his brother moved in with his sister. He pays half the mortgage on his sister's house and still bosses everybody around. Tony took charge of the insurance adjusters and the contractors who are rebuilding their house. That may take a long time, but Tony listens a bit more now, and sometimes he even allows his brother and sister to have their say. Facing your anger and sense of being alone is the first step toward reconnecting with the people you love.

———

If we have siblings, it is inevitable that we'll either be mourned first or will do the mourning. Surviving brothers and sisters can help us in a way that no one else can. With them, there is no taboo about getting together to talk, reminisce, and express sorrow, anger, and guilt. With them, childhood stories are treasured, and tears are accepted. With them, even acting like a child again can be understood in the context of mourning. The Kinsons have been unusually close brothers and sisters from the time they were little, and I believe that their connections with one another have sustained them through tragedy and kept them laughing when times are good.

KNITTING TOGETHER

It's a family of six brothers and sisters, three pairs born close to each other over nearly two decades. They grew up poor, in a tiny two-bedroom house in a very small town in the Midwest. None of the kids could take a bath in privacy before school, because their clothes closet was in the bathroom. This really bugged the youngest brother, the most difficult member of the clan.

He was always trouble—or in trouble. The third and last boy, Randy got short shrift. The year he had ringworm, which was treated with a smelly rub on a shaved head, Randy hid out in the doghouse to keep from getting on the school bus. He was not a happy kid, and he tortured his littlest sisters. He would tie them up and spit on them, and tell them scary stories. To this day one of the sisters—nearly fifty now—sleeps with a blanket over her head. Randy and his father were at odds. The oldest sister describes a scene in the kitchen, of her father sitting on Randy's chest and just hitting him and hitting him. She always came to his aid, trying to protect him as best she could—this was one of her missions in life.

Tall and handsome, Randy was the image of their father. He set high school track records but never did well academically. He was popular with the girls and wholly irresponsible. When he got his high school girlfriend pregnant (he was eighteen and she was sixteen), they married and lived in a trailer in the Kinsons' backyard. Randy couldn't keep a job, and he had a hard time managing his temper. His wife often had bruises or a sprained wrist. It broke Randy's heart when she left him, taking the kids (there were two sons by then). The sisters worried when he threatened to kill himself. They tiptoed around their troubled brother, but he pulled himself together.

Randy soon recovered and married a beautiful and gifted woman, a musician. They had two daughters. But when the financial problems worsened, his temper got the best of him, and he started having affairs. When this wife also left him, taking their two daughters, Randy was devastated. Again, he threatened to kill himself, the family worried, and again he recovered.

Women couldn't keep away from Randy, even though he was violent and unfaithful. His younger sister went so far as to warn the woman who turned out to be the third wife, "You do not want to marry my brother. He is not good for women; he's not good for himself. You don't want to do this." The woman wouldn't listen: "Oh, I know, I know. But I love him." This wife brought Randy's children back into the family, but over the years, their financial troubles mounted, and so did Randy's odd behavior. His eldest daughter remembers driving by the house: "He's out front wearing his cutoff shirt, and he's got this thing of blue paint. He's taking this blue paint on the big sidewalk squares out in front of the house, and he'd written in big letters a big L, a big O, and a big V, and he was working on the E. It was, like, LOVE, and it was huge, all the way up to the door." She said, "What are you doing?" He looked up from the sidewalk. "I'm reminding people what it's all about, darlin', reminding people what it's all about." His daughter pauses, then says, "That moment when he looked over at me, he had the best eye wrinkles. When he laughed, man, his eyes laughed louder than his voice did, and I will remember him looking over at me and laughing, and then giving me a 'Take what I'm saying seriously' kind of look."

When his third wife left him, Randy was mortified, and he didn't talk about it. His middle sister tells me, "He came to our house one day and brought me this big houseplant, said, 'I want you to have this.' He said, 'I'm moving out of the house, me and Ginny have separated.' " She was shocked but not surprised and said, "Oh, Randy, that's terrible. Is there anything we can do?" There was nothing they could do. When he called his daughter, she heard something in his voice. "Don't do it, Daddy," she pleaded. He told her he loved her and said good-bye. His older sister got anxious that night, because she hadn't heard from him all day. She and her boyfriend drove around to his house and found the garage door down. He had done it this time. Randy was gone.

A decade later, they all sit around and talk about him. The middle sister says, "It's such a shame that he can't be here to see what has transpired in his children. All four college graduates, all of them extremely bright, personable people." The oldest brother tells me, "I do have a deep-seated regret that I wasn't better able to understand our brother Randy's circumstances and situation. I just didn't; I don't understand it to this day." To this day the protector sister berates herself for not doing enough. The sister who sleeps with the blanket over her head was always judgmental of Randy, and she feels guilty about that. Even though each of the brothers and sisters has a private and personal sense of guilt and responsibility for Randy's death, together they form a group that sustains them. The group actually got a bit bigger after the funeral.

Seven years earlier, the oldest brother and his wife had divorced because of his infidelities. "I was stupid," he tells me. They, too, had married as teenagers, and she'd grown up with his brothers and sisters—they were like family to her. Of course she attended Randy's funeral; this was still her family, even if she was no longer married into it. As they were fixing up the table for the reception, her former husband said, "If you ever would be of a mind to put our family back together, call me, because I would really like to do that." He tells me, "I mean, it was obvious to me that I had really screwed things up." She said she would think about it and called him a few weeks after the funeral. They remarried later that year. The sisters tell me that their hearts are still broken because they lost Randy, but they are grateful that they got Cindy back. The girls had loved her all their lives.

The bonds among these brothers and sisters were forged in a hard childhood and renewed in the tragedy of their brother's suicide. They visit all the time, they spend holidays together, they surprise one another with birthday gifts and trips, and they look out for the nieces and nephews.

They tell me of a day when all three of Randy's ex-wives

came to visit the family. "I mean, just because you don't have the same name anymore doesn't mean that you're not family," one sister says. Randy's first wife looked around. "This is really my family, these people," she told them. "I always wanted somebody to hug me, and your family hugged each other. You're huggers. And you're kissers. And that's the reason you're my family. You make us feel part of you."

I met the Kinsons ten years after Randy's death, and their story was so vivid I felt it had happened the month before. Each of them told a slightly different version, and I began to realize that these multiple retellings gave them perspectives on their common tragedy. Different memories comfort us, stories that make us laugh are healing, and in the sharing, pain may be diminished.

Throughout human history, groups of people have sat around, telling and retelling stories of heroism and woe. It's in our nature to repeat and repeat the founding stories of our families. The Kinsons understood this, and their ability to be together, to hear and to speak, has turned them into a strong and caring clan.

Part 3

MAKING CHOICES

8

TRADING PLACES

I have always loved the expression "I'm still trying to figure out what I'm going to do when I grow up," especially when it comes from a middle-aged person. It reminds me how unfinished we all are. It also expresses great optimism: that there is plenty of time, both to grow up and to accomplish our highest goals, when we are ready. Brothers and sisters, no matter how old they may be, feel pressure to grow up fast when their parents need their help and care. This moment in life shines a bright light on siblings. During what is for many people a difficult and painful period, we have to provide for the parent's care, deal with our already busy lives, and do the hard work of beginning to say good-bye. If we are caring for the last parent, this period is a tryout for being an orphan. I don't know a person who, when the last parent goes, doesn't feel oddly and sadly alone.

———

It is hard to act like a mature adult under such pressure. Most of us fall down part of the time—we're only human. All the old patterns of our childhood emerge as we care for the elders. The brother who was a bully may try to push everybody around; the favorite may act as if whatever little she does to help is more than sufficient; the prodigal makes a twenty-four-hour appearance to wild applause from the needy parent, amid glares from the siblings who have been bearing the burden 24-7; and the martyred brother or sister who has done all the miserable work stands around with a sad face. Jealousies, rivalries, and miseries abound. In these last months or years of our parents' lives, we are extremely sensitive to our siblings' actions, the responsibilities they shoulder, and the ones they shirk. How we behave during this period can have a lasting effect, transforming our relationships in a positive or a negative way. When brothers and sisters come together to help with their parents, they form new bonds despite the travails of their childhood. Some people understand, before the passing of the last parent, that their brothers and sisters will soon be all they have of their original family, and they begin the work of reconnecting, on the phone and in hospital rooms, elder facilities, and nursing homes.

When I was a kid, we loved to play "Spy." We would write messages in lemon juice on a piece of paper and let it dry. Hold the paper over a lit candle and—presto!—the words emerge in brownish lettering. I think of that magic writing when I consider how we act with our brothers and sisters when the time comes to take responsibility for our aging parents. In some families, it seems as if the grown children were reading secret messages and following the ancient directions. So often, these messages from a long-gone past are telling the grown brothers and sisters to return to the nursery and to treat each other the way they did when they were kids.

Lois was her father's favorite, and her older sister was the one who came in for punishment when they were children, especially from their father, who was perpetually irritated with her, spanking her and criticizing her all the time. Now that their father is old and ill, Lois cannot understand why her sister refuses to help with his care. Her sister says that their father was physically abusive when she was a kid and he is not nice to her now, so why should she lift a finger for him? Let Lois, his favorite daughter, do the heavy lifting, she thinks.

TIME TRAVEL

Lois remembers their weekend car trips. She and her little sister sat in the back seat, singing all the songs they knew and making up new ones, as their parents drove from their hometown to their mother's family a hundred miles away. Lois dreaded getting there, because the aunts and uncles would tease her about being her father's favorite. They all recognized that her older sister got the smacks and she got the hugs. The relatives would joke, "We'll sell tickets when Lois gets spanked." This made Lois feel terrible. It wasn't her fault that she was her father's favorite. Lois's older sister had to help out in their father's general store after school. I suspect that she took a lot of criticism there. Lois, when she appeared from time to time, was the precious little helper.

Lois doesn't remember her older sister as a bad or disruptive child, and she never could understand what she did to deserve all the yelling and spanking. Not having endured what her older sister calls abuse, Lois has no sympathy for her sister's behavior as an adult. Here's the thing about the favorite: the favorite, too young to understand what is really going on, thinks she deserves special treatment because she is doing a better job as a daughter. That's how children construe disparate treatment. Lois's older sister blamed Lois for being the favorite, which is also a child's inaccurate assessment of the situation. You can't ask a favorite child to say, "This isn't fair, Daddy, hit me instead of her." But over time, as she grew up, Lois's sister stopped blaming her and so deeply resented their father for beating up on her, that she could not forgive him.

Sixty years have passed since the long car rides, and their father is over ninety and failing. The sisters are still fighting over him— but it's not about his love; it's about his needs. He's on the treadmill of the elderly: from home to one doctor, back home, to another doctor, with intermittent phone calls to the specialists and trips to the pharmacy. Lois shoulders the vast preponderance of this burden, and her sister participates only when she must. If Lois is out of town, her sister will visit their dad, and if there is an emergency, she'll take him to the doctor. But by and large, she won't be around him. "She hates him," Lois says. "Always?" I ask. Lois nods. "She thinks Dad abused her."

Lois is agnostic about the abuse, but she is perplexed that her sister can't get over it. She tells her sister, "Okay, Daddy right now is an old man. He has dementia; he's got health issues. What can he do to harm you now?" The trouble is that her sister experiences their father the way she always has—as a brutal and cruel man. "When my sister would go to see my dad, he would yell at her," Lois tells me. Like many very old people, their father was getting paranoid. "You're taking my money, you're stealing my money," he would yell. The screaming and the craziness drove Lois's older sister up the wall. "She can't handle it," Lois says. "And so she became less and less involved because she wasn't going to be brutalized." When their father screams at Lois, she shrugs it off. "I love him and I care about him. That's the difference," Lois explains. She swears that her father treats them the same: "I have two wonderful daughters" is what he says. Listening to her, I feel as if I'm watching shadow play on the nursery wall. The elder sister is still furious at her father, and the younger believes her sister is still a bad daughter. Ever the good daughter, Lois bears most of the burden for the care of their father, and her eyes narrow when she talks about her wayward sister.

I met their father, a natty fellow hunched over with age and sporting a cabbie's cap. Charming and very hard of hearing, this polite gentleman of ninety-three didn't look scary at all—a feather could blow him over. But age and fragility don't make him less frightening to Lois's sister. She grew up under the cloud of his temper and she watched Lois bask in his approval.

Lois tells me about an incident that took place at a restaurant where they had their father out for lunch. The elder sister was anxious about his mental state and kept at him, repeatedly asking him what day it was, who was president, and so forth. This got on Lois's nerves, and she told her sister to stop the questioning. The barrage continued. Finally, in a rage, Lois did what her father had so often done to this sister—she swatted her. That was it, for a long time.

A year later, their father passed away, at the age of ninety-four. Maybe now that her father is gone, Lois's sister's anger will subside. And without their unequal burdens, the sisters won't have daily cause to be irritated at each other. They might even relax into an easier relationship. Or the differences between their personalities and styles will still rankle and keep them from being close. There's no guarantee that when the offending parent dies, the siblings will close ranks and become dear friends. Life isn't that simple.

Sometimes brothers and sisters give each other happy surprises. A friend of mine told me about her youngest brother. He lives across the country and doesn't visit their father much, but he has taken over responsibility for his finances and business affairs. My friend finds this tremendously helpful—she has her hands full with her own family and her job, as well as visiting their dad every day in the elder-care facility near her home. My friend isn't good with paperwork and money, and she doesn't know what she would do without her brother's help. He is six years her junior, and she never thought to rely on him when they were kids. Now her face shines with the discovery of her little brother's strengths and kindness.

Happy surprises from brothers and sisters you never really knew as kids are nice. But imagine what it feels like when a brother you never cared for steps up to the plate, odd personality and all.

THE EVIL TWIN

Wayne, a large and comfy-looking man nearing sixty, has a brother he never got along with. He and his older sister and younger brother are fine together. But this one brother—a fraternal twin—is just plain hard to be around, and he is different from his brothers and sisters. He is conservative, whereas they are liberal; he is overbearing, whereas they are reserved; and he is wealthy, while they are just comfortable. This brother was always difficult. He and their father were constantly at odds, and he made trouble in school. Even though they were twins, these brothers were as different as two family members can be. After all, fraternal twins share no more than the other siblings—except their birth date. As he grew up, Wayne came to realize that this brother prefers to be oppositional.

This brother still enjoys getting under his siblings' skin. Wayne's sister is a community organizer, and his brother calls her a Commie. Wayne's little brother has become an observant Jew, and the tough brother treats religion with contempt. The only sibling he is nice to, in fact, is Wayne, whom he barks at plenty but also admires. Wayne now thinks that his brother takes after their mother. She is also stubborn. This last quality serves her well—when you're ninety years old, being stubborn can be a survival strategy. She knows how to get what she needs. And the impossible brother takes care of her—in his inimitable way.

After their father died, her children decided to move their mother from the family home to an elder-care facility. The Orthodox brother suggested a nice place near him in Florida; the political sister offered a garden apartment near her in Atlanta; and Wayne found her a good situation near him in Boston. But their rich brother didn't wait. He placed her in a luxury facility near him on the Connecticut River—and he's paying for it. Their mother was born in the Bronx and likes living in New England, so she was happy to land there.

Still, Wayne can't stop his brother's grousing. He tells me that when he calls and says he's planning to visit Mom, the brother says, "Don't come." When he says he's sending her something she needs, he says, "Don't bother." His brother is mean about their mother now, and his difficult personality still rubs Wayne the wrong way. But when his mother phoned Wayne to complain that his twin brother was trying to poison her, he knew that she was getting a little senile. His brother was no murderer. Wayne and his other brother and sister may still express the old patterns of annoyance, but they appreciate their difficult brother's efforts, even if he can be a royal pain. This family is acting out the old drama, but the difficult brother has stepped up to support their mother, and the others are grateful.

I know a woman who was her mother's least favorite child. She never got the approval or the attention her brothers and sisters did. Even so, this busy career person with children and grand-children was the one who stepped up and moved her elderly mother to a facility near her. She visits her mom on the way home from work nearly every day and brings the great-grand-children to visit on weekends. She makes the decisions about health care and hospitalization, and she deals with the staff at the facility. She does her mother's laundry. Over the years of daily visits, she began to experience her mother's trust and approval, and she gradually stopped being annoyed at her sib-lings for being less attentive. I think the hole in her heart that came from being the child who got the least attention was finally filled, as she began to experience her mother's gratitude and love. When the other children visit, her mother tries to rise to the occasion, even when she isn't feeling so good. When my friend visits, her mom turns over and gives a sigh—of relief and recognition. Sometimes she feels well enough to chat with her daughter, but if she doesn't, that is also okay. This woman always knew that she had to try harder to get her mom's affec-tion. She did it, and eventually it worked.

Is it possible that we ignore the benefits of being the least favorite child and fail to recognize the burden placed on the favorite? The story of Debra and her sisters is a lesson about the legacy of favoritism.

THE PARAGON VANISHES

"Why can't you be like her?" That was Debra's mother's refrain. Debra's oldest sister, eleven years her senior, was perfection. This daughter did exactly what their mother wished: cleaned her room before school, curled her hair for church by the age of seven, wore makeup and dressed properly in order to make her mother proud when she was a teenager. She married young (never finished college) and had children right away—the very model of the 1950s daughter. Debra, the youngest of three girls, wished she could be just like her, but she was too much of a rebel, and growing up eleven years after her sister she lived in a different America. Debra dressed like a hippie (she still does), tried to get out of going to church, and worked her way through college. Debra's oldest sister was even more judgmental than their parents, and she could be unkind. Take the Sunday afternoon Debra and a boyfriend came home after a weekend at the shore. "Here come the little sinners," her sister commented. She was a perfectionist and accepted no deviation.

The oldest sister was never close to her younger sisters, who couldn't help but roll their eyes at her perfection. When she and her family moved an hour's drive away, this sister invested all her energy in her husband, her children, and her community. She was a dedicated church member who cared for the ill and needy in her parish. Her charity did not extend to home.

When it came to helping with the care of their parents, she

disappeared. During the months of their father's steep decline and early death, she just would not pitch in. It was too much for her, she said. The two younger sisters took over and cared for their dying father. Several years after his death, their mother suffered a series of strokes. At first she was able to live by herself and just push an emergency button when she needed help, but after a while she required round-the-clock care. After her insurance ran out their mother needed 24-7 care, which they could not afford. It was up to the daughters to care for their mother. It was a miserable situation.

By this time Debra had moved thousands of miles away and had a job, a husband, and a small child. With the oldest sister out of the picture, the burden fell on Debra's middle sister. She had a business to run and two small kids; her life became a nightmare. Debra flew home once a month and gave her relief, but that was not sufficient. They needed their older sister, and she said she couldn't pitch in. Her kids were grown by then, and she was caring for a church member who was no worse off than her own mother. Why was she unwilling or unable to help? She never gave them a satisfactory answer, and so they concluded that she "just doesn't get it" and never will. This is an expression I have heard many times over the course of my interviews. I have come to see that when a brother or sister "just doesn't get it" or "lives in a bubble," he or she has closed the door to honest conversation. It means that the natural back-and-forth of disagreement and coming together is not wanted or warranted. When bubble siblings keep their feelings to themselves, they have nothing much to share with their brothers and sisters. There's usually a reason for this, but bubble siblings don't tell.

Here's one thought experiment that imagines how this sister might explain her behavior. Perhaps she didn't particularly like being the paragon all her life. She may have told herself that as a child she met all the requirements her parents set down, and she lived the life they wanted for her, in that old 1950s way. She serves her church and her family with devotion. But she never had the opportunities offered her younger sisters, who were never her friends; she knew they resented her, but she was just following the rules. It is not always fun to be held up as the model daughter—that puts burdens on a person, burdens she never shared with her siblings. It's not her fault, she may think, that Debra moved thousands of miles away, or that the middle sister has a career and children; they made their own choices. "So let them bear the burden," she might be thinking. "I gave at home when I was young." This imagined defense may be plausible or not, but the other sisters never heard any defense, and they are furious.

Debra tells me that her middle sister, the one who bore the brunt, cannot be in the same room with her older sister. "Is there anything she could do to make you forgive her?" I ask, struck by the finality of judgment. "I doubt it," Debra answers. I pursue this: "If she were to talk to you both and say, 'I really was wrong, and I'm sorry'—or is just that unthinkable?" Debra is adamant: "If it registered and she did it, then we'd both forgive her, we would be fine. But it's unthinkable that her brain would operate that way." Whatever was going through the oldest sister's mind during the years when she did not participate in the care of the parents, she has isolated herself from her sisters. Debra's narration of this story carries a sense of surprise and disappointment, which adds to her anger. Unhappy surprises about brothers and sisters at the end of a parent's life are searing and can leave permanent scars. Happy surprises do the opposite.

———

It took Janice until she was a grown woman to see her little sisters as people. She had been their big sister–mother, and so they were always little girls to her. This changed when their mother took ill. The mutual respect and love that grew in the years that followed has grown into a deep and abiding connection.

SATURDAYS WITH MOMMA

It's a warm spring day and I am on the porch of a small building across from the house where Janice and her brothers and sisters grew up. I'm enjoying my ride on a wooden swing that is suspended by chains from the porch ceiling. We're drinking iced tea and waiting for the lasagna to cook through. Janice's younger sister is making us a delicious country dinner later this evening. The porch is a place where everybody hangs out. It has been that way since they were kids. Mima, their maternal grandmother, lived in this little cottage until she died. They adored her. The youngest sister used to have nightmares, and in the middle of the night she would creep across the yard to Mima's and crawl into her bed. Just before dawn, when she was ready to go home, Mima would get up, too, and sit by the window. Mima would watch her cross the yard and wave to her when she arrived back at her own door.

There were six children in this family. Janice is the oldest girl, and her two younger sisters came along eleven and twelve years later. She was like a mother to them. They adored her. "We watched her put on makeup. We watched her go out on dates," they say. The two sisters are animated in their description of how much they idolized Janice. She is quiet and listens with her head tilted to one side.

Janice is in her mid-fifties. Even in jeans and a man's shirt, this woman has style. "She was a cheerleader in high school, and very, very well liked, and had lots and lots of friends, and we tagged along, probably because she had to drag us along," adds the middle sister, the one who makes things happen—including tonight's lasagna. I ask Janice how this felt. "I was kind of like Mom," she says. "Mom worked. They had to get up, they had to get dressed, and they had to go to school. The beds had to be made before you left, always, or you rushed home to make sure they were made before Mother got home." The littlest sister interrupts: "She had good-looking boyfriends. We always had crushes on her boyfriends."

The two youngest girls were born a year apart and raised together, tussling and teasing each other constantly. Janice was their referee. Janice got married when her sisters were ten and eleven, and she pretty much left the family after that. It turns out that the reason for Janice's disappearing act was her husband, who wanted her all for himself. Janice eventually divorced this man and married a high school beau. Happily, the girls got Janice back.

The two youngest girls were always close. The youngest sister is quiet. Her two older sisters testify that she is the kindest and least judgmental woman on the planet. Small and wiry, she sits on the porch with a knit stole wrapped around her shoulders. She seems to be both protecting herself and keeping warm under her wrap. She has a honeyed voice and doesn't say much, but her face is full of feeling. The two younger sisters regale me with stories that show how much they love Janice, who nods in appreciation. Then the conversation shifts. It's Janice's turn. She looks into the middle distance and starts talking:

"It wasn't until after Mommy got sick and I had an opportunity to spend as much time as I did with them, that I really did bond with them." Now I hear about the formation of their relationships as adults. When their mother was in her fifties, she endured a number of small strokes. Her language and memory were intact, but she lost her energy. Soon she could not care for herself, their father was wearing out, and they worried for his health. The six children had to decide what to do about their mother, whom they adored. She was tough about chores, and she had high standards, but she was the stable element in their lives. They admired her energy and smarts, and they were determined to take good care of her.

After much discussion, they agreed that it was time to move their mother into the local nursing home. They went as a group to tell their parents. Nobody was happy. Their mother was devastated but eventually agreed, understanding the toll her illness was taking on her husband. Their father was so angry that he sat on the very swing where I heard this story, with a shotgun on his lap, threatening them while they were taking her away. This was one of the most painful days in the life of the family, but it was softened by the promise her daughters made.

The sisters would bring her home every weekend and spend Saturdays in the kitchen, and they would take her back to the nursing home on Sunday. They bought a hospital bed for the living room, so she could sleep there, and they dragged a big, comfortable chair into the kitchen. There was a precedent for their Saturdays. When the kids were growing up, their beloved Mima and their mother and assorted aunts would gather in their tiny kitchen on Saturdays and gossip and do their nails, and have a fine time.

So the ritual came to life again. Either on Friday afternoon or

Saturday morning, the middle sister would drive to the nursing home and pick up their mother, putting the wheelchair in the back of the van. The other sisters would be home by the time they got back. First, they would give their mother a shower and check for bedsores (the middle sister visited her every Wednesday to wash her and check for sores, too), and then they would dry her and dress her in a soft robe or jogging suit. Hair and nails were next. I asked if they dyed her hair. They let it go white. "But we used gel, and sometimes we gave her a pixie cut," the middle sister says, a grin on her face. They gave one another manicures, and had lunch. After their mother's nap, other family members might drop by. Dinner, TV, and then she would go to sleep in the hospital bed.

The girls promised to do this every Saturday, and they did, with few exceptions—an occasional graduation or some other important event. Their mother looked forward to these outings, and she was fine about going back to the home if she stayed only one night with her daughters. If she spent two nights at home, she would clutch the sides of her bed to keep from being taken away, because she hated to leave. Nobody expected their mother to live very long, with all these strokes. But she lasted another eight years. Think of it. Eight years of Saturdays dedicated to their ailing mom.

"I wouldn't have traded one Saturday for anything in the world," Janice sighs. The little sisters nod in agreement. Their oldest brother had this to say about the weekends: "Over the course of those years, I really learned a lot about my sisters' caring attitude, their willingness to always be there for Mom. It's something so small that most people probably wouldn't have noticed it, but they always checked to make sure that Mom was being attended to and tried to lend some dignity to what had become a terribly undignified situation." This tall man, who looks more like an astronaut than a retired high school principal, chokes up as he talks about what his sisters' activities meant not only to their mother but to him. Like many oldest sons, he had married and moved out of town. Those eight years of Saturdays brought him home. "My sisters are extraordinary people," he says. There's no way he could have known that when they were young. He was married and raising his own family when they were still small. Like Janice, he saw them as kids—burdens that older siblings have to bear.

Sitting on the swing, listening to the sisters tell me how much they loved those Saturdays with their mom, I got a glimpse of what happens when brothers and sisters shoulder their responsibilities together. The Saturdays in the kitchen began in their childhood with their mother and Mima. But their shared determination to bring their mother home for all those years brought out the best in these people, and it cemented their relationship for life.

Today, with their mother long buried, they talk on the phone all the time and take every opportunity to be together. There's an annual festival in their town in the fall, and everybody turns up. Sisters, cousins, aunts, in-laws, and former in-laws all come by to get their hugs from this embracing family. They plan for the six months before the festival, and they talk about it for the six months after. This is another occasion for them to reminisce about the eight years of Saturdays with Momma, and they do it because those memories are among their happiest.

9

MESSAGE IN A BOTTLE

Why is it that brothers and sisters so often go ballistic about the division of the estate of the last parent? I know a pair who didn't speak for years over a Tiffany lamp; he swiped it from their mother's house, and the sister who took care of the mother had always pictured it on her hall table. A woman I know cleaned out her mother's apartment in the day it took for her brother to fly to the funeral—and she packed a carton for him and his family. It contained all the things they had given the mother over the years, and nothing else, no mementos, no family pictures—just old gifts returned to sender. I remember another friend's fury when she recounted the battle with her sister over their mother's watch. Everybody knows about such fights—and writing about them makes me realize how silly they are. Childish? Absolutely. When our last parent dies, we are propelled back into the nursery.

Losing the last parent is one of the hardest times in our lives. For mourning brothers and sisters, the task of breaking up the parent's home and distributing the possessions is especially painful. We watch as their lives and our childhoods disappear before our eyes. In this supersensitive time, people feel as if they have been orphaned and often go back to square one with their siblings. Every little bit of unfairness that happened between them bubbles to the surface. Alliances that were formed in the nursery emerge again, with renewed strength.

The period after the death of the last parent is twilight for the children; the family may reconstruct itself as a community of brothers and sisters. Or they may enter a new phase of distance and dissolution. This is, after all, the first opportunity for siblings to behave toward each other as they like, without parental supervision or judgment. The brother who swiped the lamp from his mother's house might not have packed it up in front of his mom, and the sister who didn't give her brother one childhood memento might have included some family snapshots if her mother had been watching. We have seen people wait until the last parent dies to get back at the sibling who offended, or who hurt, or who was not helpful enough at the end. People who were not close but put up some kind of a front for the parents are now free to depart the family, and others whose conflict was related to the parent may now be more relaxed.

Too soon after the funeral comes the will. No matter what the parent may have planned, bereaved brothers and sisters have been known to respond with irrational and hurtful behavior. And if the will favors one or cuts out another, mayhem is unavoidable. Whatever the size of an estate, wills have lasting power. Bookshelves are filled with dramas of wealthy families in which the brothers and sisters have fought over the division of their inheritance, and I am not going to rehash these epics. Interviewing people of modest means, and hearing their stories, I have come to understand that the will of the last surviving parent can act like a time-release capsule that has significance far beyond the value of the property. It can cement closeness or send people away from each other for good.

If we find it hard to fathom the will's intent, we cannot ever know the thinking behind it: the person who devised it is in the ground. Still, the one thing we know is that when a will causes disputes, the brothers and sisters rarely blame the writer of the will—they more often blame each other. People in the grips of grief are irrational, and the conflicts that emerge at the reading of the will can bowl them over. Most people have a hard time rising above their own interests and putting away old conflicts. I met some young people who plan to approach this moment remembering the lessons they learned from observing their parents, aunts, and uncles.

THE SISTERS' PROMISE

A couple of years ago I spoke at a commencement, and I sat with the graduates at their celebration lunch. I told them about this book, and a number of them spoke up. Their grandparents were dying off, and some of the women had watched in horror as their parents and their aunts and uncles fought over the property. One said that after her mom and her aunt sued each other over their mother's estate, she and her sister pledged that their relationship would always be more important than objects. Others at the lunch table nodded; the passing of their grandparents had given them the opportunity to observe their parents' behavior, and they were more than distressed—they were uncomprehending. These young people in their twenties and thirties are idealistic, and they don't have the responsibilities of adulthood, but they were clear: there isn't anything on earth more important than their sisters and brothers, no matter what their parent's will directs. Maybe memory will fade, and when the time comes they, too, will fight over lamps and jewelry, as well as money and property. But then again, maybe they won't. We are capable of learning, and the experience of watching your parental family fall apart provides a powerful lesson.

I heard this again from a young woman in her thirties who had watched her father suffer from what she considers the treachery of his sisters. Her father and his three siblings were close. Their mother had died young, and the two brothers were pretty much raised by their two older sisters. The patriarch had started a business many years before, which supported the family in some degree of comfort. When he visited my friend's family, Grandpa offered to leave the entire business to her father, to help provide care for their handicapped daughter. Her father refused this offer, saying it wasn't fair to his brother and sisters. And so Grandpa agreed to divide his estate equally among the four children.

Years later, Grandpa was failing, and his four children moved him into a facility where he would be well cared for in his declining years. They decided to share the expenses, each paying for a month in rotation. My friend's dad suggested that they check the will, just to make sure that everything was in order, since the old man was falling into dementia. When he read the document, he was astonished and devastated. His father had written a new will that made his two sisters the sole inheritors. He and his brother had been cut out. This man's daughter tells me, "It was a complete shock. Both of these women had always gotten along with everybody." Like most siblings, the brothers blamed their sisters instead of their father. Their father was too far gone to change the will or to explain himself, so the men believed that their sisters had colluded with their dad to cut them out of the will. One of the sisters died soon after the father, and the surviving sister refuses to talk about this.

The aunts and uncles all had beach cottages next to each other and the cousins had grown up together, vacationing at the shore every summer. When the will became known, the family fell apart, and the brothers stopped talking to their sisters. What about the cousins? "They don't know why their mother did it. They're not saying their mom was wrong. They're not saying she was right. They love their mom. So they assume she had some reason, but they have no explanation." My friend hopes that her father and his sister will reconcile after the old man dies. "My guess is that during the funeral, she's going to say something, and my father will say, Okay, let's move on." My friend has tried to convince her father to open the subject with his sister, but he refuses. He thinks it's her responsibility to explain herself.

Maybe as their father was declining, he made his daughters the same offer his son had refused—and they agreed, or the father insisted. Or perhaps the father didn't consult any of his children; he was getting a bit dotty at that time and may have just decided for himself without any consultation. Whatever may have happened, the family is dissolving before everyone's eyes.

My young friend and her siblings have made a pact. "As horrible as it is and has been for my father, it actually was sort of a good moment for me and my brothers to talk to each other and say, We can never let this happen." Children watch their parents, taking lessons from every detail of their behavior. As a result, young people who see the parental generation falling apart over their inheritance are clear: It won't happen here, they pledge.

A last will and testament is primarily about how we leave our property; a legacy concerns the state in which we leave our children. Even with a parent's best intentions, grown siblings may find reason to quibble and fight. All the old issues come up again, and competition for goods is nothing compared to competition for love. Parents have a right to leave their property as they desire, but if they are not mindful of the relationships among their children, they can create conflict for generations. We cannot ask a deceased parent what they intended, but an unfortunate will can leave a stamp of discord that may never be forgotten.

Danny comes from a complicated family of seven biological children and two adopted kids. His father was a brilliant engineer and inventor, clear and organized in his work. But when it came to his family, he loved chaos, and he needed to be the center of things. Long after his death, the pot is still boiling.

MUSICAL CHAIRS

Danny is still in shock about what happened between his brothers and sisters after his father's death. All his life, his father seemed to enjoy making trouble among his children. He encouraged their competition and had a way of choosing a favorite and then rejecting him or her, only to pick a new pet for a while. Danny, as the youngest, never participated in the game; he watched as if through binoculars. As a result of his distance, he says, "I'm the only one who speaks to everybody." His father was always playing his daughters and his wife against each other and pretty much left his first son and last son out of it. But when he adopted a pair of teenaged brothers who'd had trouble in their foster homes, they added to the chaos. As Danny describes it, "You go to my house for Thanksgiving or Christmas, and there's thirty people running around screaming and I'm cooking dinner for the family. I started when I was about fourteen. I loved it, but those holidays were mayhem and it was just nuts around the family." Danny reversed the old saying: when he couldn't stand the heat, he went into the kitchen.

The game was well ensconced into the family culture when Danny's oldest sister, who did not always get along with their father, asked him to invest in a restaurant so that she could run it. Danny smelled trouble, and he told his sister, "That could possibly be the worst thing you could ever do in your life." His sister said, "Why is that?" "You are not comfortable around your father and now you want to work for him? He's going to own that restaurant, and you're not." Danny's gloomy prediction underestimated the trouble that was to come.

Within a year, the founding daughter was fired and replaced by her sister. Then she was let go, replaced by the middle brother. The pleasant Italian restaurant could have been named the Revolving Door, because for the next years one sibling would be put in charge, and then another. When the ousted sister or brother would return to favor, the former favorite would be on the street. Two sisters and one brother played musical chairs for the rest of their father's life.

Danny and an older brother had long ago pulled themselves out of the fray. But all the others were mired in tension and anxiety. Accusations flew across the generations, lawsuits were threatened, and the siblings couldn't seem to find a sensible distance from their compelling—and infuriating—father. Then he died suddenly.

After the funeral, they gathered at the lawyer's office to hear the will. The sister who was in their father's good graces at the moment inherited the restaurant and was named sole executor of the estate. The two siblings who were out of favor were disinherited altogether. Danny realized what was going on. He turned to the attorney and said, "Do you have any idea what you just did to this family?" The lawyer didn't respond. It wasn't the lawyer's responsibility, of course; he was following his client's instructions. Danny turned to the sister who'd gotten the restaurant and asked, "Do you realize that if you accept the responsibility of being sole executor and the ownership of the largest asset in the estate as it currently stands, you will not speak to any of your siblings again? It effectively shuts you off from everybody." She didn't respond, but Danny was again prophetic.

The brother who was cut out was devastated, and the disinherited sister sued the estate; the case took years to be settled. By that time the estate was bankrupt. The brothers and sisters have never recovered. They don't speak to each other, only to Danny, and he isn't happy with the situation. The only inheritance he wanted was his father's letter opener. "I have it in my hand right now. I still use it," he told me. I guess Danny should not have been so amazed by the events that took place after his father's death. The pattern of competition and conflict had been laid down for decades, and as his brothers and sisters grew up, they were unable to resist the give-and-take of their father's love and wealth. We create our earthly immortality in the memories we leave our children and those close to us. Danny's father left a legacy of disruption. But that is not the only kind a parent can leave. A mother living thousands of miles away from her grown sons also left her mark.

A MOTHER'S WISH

I met a man from Turkey who has lived in this country for twenty years; his four brothers have also emigrated over the decades. They all worked hard to create a life for themselves and their families here. It has been hard, but they are making it now. Their mother, who died a year ago, never came to America, but the sons visited her regularly—as time and money allowed. In between visits, they phoned her every week, and they spoke about their lives to the elderly woman who sat in a small house in a small Turkish village. She must have been a wise one, because she could hear beneath the words: her sons did not get along. Old rivalries and new betrayals kept them at odds. Sometimes a pair of brothers would bond for a while, but then they would fall away from each other, and another temporary alliance would form. Jamal tells me that he got to the point where he didn't trust his brothers and he was happy to be separated from them. By then they lived all over the country. Jamal and his brothers didn't have the energy for their strife and troubles.

This is how it was until their mother took ill. The trips home became more frequent, and each of the brothers began contemplating, with great sadness, the loss of their mother. They may not have cared for each other, but they loved her. As her condition worsened, they took to phoning her more often. Their mother knew that her death was approaching, and so she spoke to each of her sons. She begged them to reconnect. She urged them to get back in touch, even if they didn't feel like it. Her moral authority was not diminished as her life ebbed, and she exacted a promise from each of them.

After her death, Jamal tells me, they gradually began to follow her wishes. One would call the other, and the brothers who lived near each other would occasionally visit. Somehow, as they spent time eating together, reminiscing, and seeing the children get to know one another, their old antagonisms began to fade. Gradually these brothers connected with each other and rebuilt the structure their mother had created so long ago. The idea of an ethical will, as well as a financial one, is gaining popularity. I doubt that their mother, living in her Turkish village, knew about this trend, but she understood that, having lost her sons to a new country, she couldn't let them lose each other.

Even in a very large family where the conflict among the children is a constant source of energy and anger, it is possible for brothers and sisters to rise to the occasion. The children in Roger's family are lucky to be the inheritors of some beautiful objects, but most importantly, they had a brother who recognized the right thing, who did the right thing, and who helped them all find their better selves.

PORTRAIT OF POPPY

Imagine a big old creaky house near the shore. It was the home of ten children, two parents, and, for many years, two grandparents. The grandparents had moved in when child six arrived and their daughter, the mother, was totally overwhelmed. Her husband was a beautiful man, spiritual, emotionally connected, and they used to say, "He was born with every gift, save ambition." There was not much money, and there were plenty of mouths to feed, but their mother convinced all of them that money didn't matter; people did. Fourteen people sat down to dinner every night. Father carved, Mother dished out the food, and the plates were passed down the table. The oldest brother was known to say, "Oh my God, there's an airplane landing right outside." As the little kids would run to the window, he'd take half their food. They stole from each other regularly. Roger tells me, "I had a part-time job when I was in high school, and I would buy a nice shirt. My brother would steal it and sometimes sell it to a friend. My sisters would steal from each other a lot; they'd sneak in and take each other's clothes and stuff like that. If you had any candy or sweets, you had to hide it. I still hide things!" His older sister, a teacher, has that habit to this day. She admits, "I'll go into the lounge at school. See who's around at nine or so, check out the cookies, put some in my lunch bag—and eat them at leisure."

They fought all the time. How else could it be? No parent could supervise all the kids. Roger recollects, "We had a standard phrase in the family, and you just filled in the name: 'Blank hit me as hard as he could for no reason at all.'" The family had a myth that was useful in controlling violence, he explains: "If you hit somebody really hard in the middle of the back, they'll get polio (which is totally absurd). So we all believed that. During a fight, somebody would inevitably get hit in the middle of the back, and would immediately do this beautiful act." That child would collapse slowly on the ground, moaning, "I can't breathe! I can't move!" The kid who'd done the hitting would think, "Oh my God, I gave my sister (or brother) polio."

Polio was a terrible disease in those years. In fact, the oldest son suffered from it, and it was to help out with him and the rest of the kids that the grandparents had moved in. This boy adored Poppy. All the children did. "When you came home from school, you each had a moment with him alone," Roger remembers. They never had to share their time with Poppy, "He'd always have a little treat for you, a doughnut, cheese and crackers, and you got to sit down and talk to him by yourself." For a family as large as this, with parents living under siege from their brood, Poppy, with his Irish wit and his big heart, helped every one of those kids grow up feeling known and loved. They all treasured the portrait a famous painter had done of Poppy; they loved that painting almost as much as they loved him. After he died, it went to the second son, who took it home.

As they grew up and moved away, the youngest daughter stayed in their town. When their mother was diagnosed with a fatal form of cancer, this sister contacted her siblings. "I do not want you to worry about Dad," she told them, "because I'm going to move in when Mother dies." She and her husband did (they had no children), and they cared for their father for a decade. The first years were fine, but as dementia set in, things were not so easy. The brothers and sisters would come home from time to time, but they didn't assume responsibility for the father, and they were grateful to this sister for her hard work.

Their father died, having left his small trust equally divided among the ten kids, but there was a CD he had forgotten to cash in, and it was worth $60,000. "A fight almost erupted at the time. There were a few family heirlooms," Roger tells me. "You could see there was a flurry of e-mails and phone calls," and people were saying things like, "Mom said she wanted this portrait to go to So-and-So, and you know, I just don't feel right about that." As all the unresolved old issues reappeared, Roger describes this moment of tension among the brothers and sisters: "You are pining for your parents. You are pining for the love that you didn't get while you were growing up. Also, that sibling jealousy, which you can never avoid, is there." They were preparing to go home and meet about the division of their father's property when the brother who had been named executor wrote them all a letter. It said, in part, "I am feeling this energy coming up, and I just want you to know that these are things. They are not as important as relation-ships. So, let's go in with that spirit." This brother owned the portrait of Poppy, and he knew that his older brother, the one who'd had polio as a kid and had been the first grandchild, pined for it. "But," says Roger, "he didn't want to be pushy about asking for it."

They all returned to the old house. Before the big meeting took place they gathered at the cemetery, to inter their father's ashes next to their mother. The oldest son had stopped by Poppy's grave, and that is where my friend Roger found him. "He was standing over my grandfather's grave and he was weeping," Roger says. Roger put his arm around his brother and discovered that his tears were a mixture of sorrow and grat-itude. "He gave me that portrait of Poppy," Roger's brother told him. His younger brother had brought the portrait with him, so he could see his brother's face when he presented it to him. Roger did something similar, he says: "I had decided that I didn't want a ring I had gotten from my mother's first cousin. I gave it to one of my sisters who did not get a promised ring from my mother." Another sister realized that the Art Deco mirror she'd had for twenty years actually belonged to her younger brother.

Before they met to dismantle the house and divide up the valuables, they had one more big decision. It was about the CD that was to be split into ten parts. Perhaps the youngest sister, who had cared for their father for a decade, should receive the entire amount. The executor brother suggested that they come to him individually and tell him what they wished. If any of them wanted his or her rightful share, he would cash it in and divide it up. If they agreed unanimously to give it to their sister, that's what would happen. Roger continues the story: "I was the final vote. No one said divide it. Everyone said give it to Arlene."

Then it was time to start the division of property. "This is how we're going to do it," they agreed. "We're going to go around and everybody can say what they want." One of the sisters said, "I really want those Ralph Waldo Emerson books." Another sister said, "I do, too, but why don't you go ahead and take them." It went like that. The sisters kept giving each other gifts from the estate. The boys didn't care about any of that stuff. They trooped into their father's bedroom and started looking at the "coffee-stained ties, and the size 17AAA shoes." Roger said, "All I want is one pair of his shoes." Somebody else said, "I'll take his old shaving kit." Roger continues, "My sisters in the other room were just screaming with delight and laughing." A few weeks later, one of the girls decided to give her sister a set of silverware she had taken, and the first editions of Hawthorne and Dickens passed from sibling to sibling.

Here is their true legacy: a phenomenal grandfather; loving parents who were too busy to supervise them and get into their disputes; a code of honor among them; and an ability to fight and make up. "If we hadn't fought and lived through the fights, we would not have recognized what my brother reminded us of, which is that these things are things, and our relationships are not."

I asked one sister if they are still close. "How do you define close?" she asked. I responded with a question: "I don't know how to define close. Why don't you?" "Well, some people say you talk frequently, which we don't at all." Okay, then what is it? "I think when we do talk, the years disappear, but not in a sense that we want to go back to the old relationship. If I haven't talked to you in months, it doesn't make any difference. You know I love you. You can talk about whatever you want to talk about." That's about as good a definition as you can find.

So long as our parents are well and functioning, we can't help having them in mind as we interact with our siblings. It's as if they have moved to the back seat of the family car and are watching us deal with our siblings. We imagine their reactions as if we're catching them in the rearview mirror. But when they are gone, the back seat is empty, and we are free to decide whether or not to ride together with our brothers and sisters. Men and women who never cared for their siblings may finally decide to separate for good, now that their parents are no longer present to be disappointed or hurt. Others may reevaluate their relationships, now that the family is shrinking. Some siblings find a release from the impact of their parents, who may have been unwitting irritants between them and their siblings.

———

We don't have to make these decisions immediately. First, we need to emerge from the childhood we once shared, and to let our feelings about our siblings mature. Then we can decide about how close we want to be. We may savor the good memories and jettison the bad—this is a function of age. We can decide to let the past go and work on a revived closeness, or we can opt for the Wedding and Wake relationship so many people prefer. And we can decide, for once and for all, to lift the burden of our siblings from our shoulders and face the world with the new families we have created. Whatever choices we make, let them be mindful, and thoughtful, and forgiving—of ourselves and of the people who formed us.

10

BUILDING TOGETHER

A friend of mine who is an artist—a tiny woman who paints enormous canvases—once said to me, "Sometimes I feel as if I'm larger on the inside than I am on the outside." She was talking about her process of painting and where she finds the source of her creativity. I love that comment, and I often think of it in relation to the arts.

But recently I have come to believe that what she said is true of us all. Most of us don't have the talent to become artists, but we all have within us enormous energy and passion. It's what we're born with, and how we related to the people in our early lives. Growing up is a matter of taming, or educating, those passions. Distancing ourselves from these emotions, we often forget what we once felt, and those powerful childhood feelings abate over time. This has many benefits; for one, it makes our lives more manageable. It's not pleasant to experience those old sentiments—the strongly positive ones scare us, and the powerfully negative ones threaten our sense that we are good people. But this process of civilization poses risks: when we shut down these feelings completely, we lose a part of ourselves.

Access to strong emotions isn't just for artists. Passionate feelings are not just directed to lovers, spouses, and partners. I think it is a part of who we are, a part of how we used to feel about our siblings—and probably still feel about them in some way. The effort to downplay these feelings has been part of our culture, which in the second half of the twentieth century favored friends over family. We can rail about our parents and complain about our kids, but how many baby boomers do you know would consider talking about their brothers and sisters in strong terms? Whatever we say or do, these feelings may be forgotten, but they are not lost, and they emerge at different times during our lives. It turns out that the less we deal with those issues as adults, the more readily they emerge when we least want them to. We can pack the sad and angry feelings with ice, but we can't make them go away forever. That energy can also propel us to face the difficulties with brothers and sisters and give us the courage to seek a resolution we can live with. Why would any adult decide to take the chance to try for a pleasant and even warm relationship with a brother or sister who has been an antagonist?

- There's the pull of memory and the desire to share (and compare) childhood with the people who lived it with us.
- Maybe it's the desire to set things right after a lifetime of conflict.
- Sometimes, when brothers and sisters become parents, they witness their children doing the eternal dance of siblings and understand some of what happened to them.

- Then there is curiosity, the desire to figure out what was really going on all those years ago.
- Some people feel a need to secure the family against the threat of dissolution.
- The search for intimacy may emerge at a time when loneliness is setting in.
- Sometimes people reconnect with brothers and sisters to maintain their sense of moral rightness.
- If we share responsibility for our aging parents, we may discover strengths in each other we never noticed.
- And sometimes people just can't bear to carry the anger and the hurt anymore.

Any or all of these reasons is sufficient to cause a person to go in search of the lost brother or sister. What's necessary for the rebuilding is a willingness on the part of both parties to contemplate the possibility of a reunion.

Turning an antagonistic relationship, or a distant one, into a friendship is hard work. Carolyn was eleven when her parents divorced, and she worried all her life about losing her sister, with whom she always had serious issues. She was nearly forty when she realized what a disaster it would be if they severed their connection, not only for her and her husband but for the baby she was carrying. She understood that it takes two to reconcile.

BEST ENEMIES

Two sisters, two years apart, always fighting, always hurting each other, the younger physically, the older emotionally. Passionately attached to each other in a negative relationship, they grew up in a beautiful old house in a Chicago suburb. A huge staircase dominated the entry hall of the house, polished to a shine by their mother, a gifted scientist who couldn't get a job once she married and had children. It was very hard for women in the sciences to make their way in their profession in the late sixties. Carolyn's mother was at home, trying to keep her self-respect and find satisfaction raising her daughters and polishing wood. To say that she wasn't present for them is to lightly sketch this woman's misery. But it had an effect on the girls, because the older sister resented being forced to share her mother's attention with the little wild beast who was foisted on her when she was two. To top it off, that infuriating little girl demanded mothering from her sister, as well.

I am speaking with the former wild beast; she is now a pioneering veterinarian who combines traditional medicine and Eastern traditions in her practice. She is a beautiful woman with a mop of curly red hair and a complexion most people would kill for. We are sitting in a garden restaurant, surrounded by chattering women with sleeping babies. I listen as we dig into the great big salads this restaurant is famous for. "I think she hated me from the minute I was born," Carolyn says. With good reason, she assures me. In a house peopled by a father who isolated himself in the study to write his great books and a distracted mother, there wasn't enough attention to go around. Carolyn admits that she was a nuisance. She couldn't stay out of her sister's space. Carolyn's early memories are peppered with smacks on her nose when her sister slammed the bedroom door to keep her out. She was always sneaking around, prying into her sister's things, and biting her older sister. The comment about biting brought a look of horror to my face. (This was an early interview for me; I discovered that biting your older sister isn't so unusual.) Carolyn explains, "It was my longing for proximity to her, deep physical urges, to be close to her. And that's why I bit her." Carolyn was remorseful, and she apologized, but that didn't help, because "in her mind I was really like a wild beast."

The famous biting incident took place when Carolyn was chasing her sister up the big staircase. She got hold of her arm and bit it as hard as she could. This was unacceptable behavior. Unfortunately, Carolyn's sister got no comfort from their parents, and no protection. She was the eldest, and instead of punishing Carolyn, they always asked, "What did you do to provoke your sister?" (Here's a moment for the older siblings reading this book to roll their eyes and nod in recognition.) Of course, the elder sister got her revenge: she was mean and rejecting; she was either critical or she acted as if this demanding little girl didn't exist.

Carolyn had a strong relationship with her stuffed animals, which may have set her on her professional course. An entourage in plush covered her bed, and a giant, people-sized stuffed dog named Mr. D. headed the high command of her imaginary army. Real dogs, despite the guardian role of Mr. D., petrified her. One day when they were all picking up clothing at the cleaners, they all overheard people discussing the tabloid newspaper story of a giant Saint Bernard that had broken out of its yard and had eaten a little boy whole, leaving only his sneakers on the pavement. Carolyn was hysterical, believing every word of the story, and she clung to her mother's arm. Her older sister rushed home ahead of them. Carolyn recalls, "She turned off all the lights in the stairwell and yelled out as I was walking up the stairs, 'Watch out, Caro, it's a dog!' and she threw Mr. D. down at me. It almost gave me a nervous breakdown." I asked if she ever forgave her sister. "I don't know if it's right to say that I never forgave her, because in my adult life, I've spent more time in therapy on my relationship with my sister than on anything else."

This childhood set the stage for these two contentious and competitive sisters. They graduated from outstanding universities and embarked on ambitious careers. Carolyn would get a stomachache when she had to spend time with her sister. When she had medical problems, her sister, now a doctor, would be adamant that Carolyn take her advice, which caused more resentment on both sides. They were never at ease with each other. Their interactions were characterized by difficult conversations and uncomfortable time spent together. They got on each other's nerves in the worst way.

At Carolyn's wedding, the hostilities reached their climax. "In front of a hundred and eighty of my close friends and family she gave this horrendous speech in which she said, 'I don't know if you all know this, but Caro bites.' " This was not a comment made in jest. "People came up to me after the wedding and said, 'Does your sister hate you?' " Carolyn shakes her head. She couldn't reply.

Carolyn never brought up the toast with her sister. She had experienced so many facets of their terrible relationship that she could see no advantage in such a conversation. There had been times when they'd lived under the same roof and hadn't spoken for months, and times in their lives when the hostilities were almost too awful to bear. Carolyn's husband has no sympathy for this sister. He's a quiet man, slow to anger, but he remembers all the misery she caused, and he doesn't forgive.

"I spent a lot of time looking into the abyss," Carolyn says. At some point, she couldn't bear it any longer—the distance and the rage were killing her. Losing her sister "would be the worst thing that I could imagine in my life."

So she began to work on it. "I really feel like I came back from the brink." It was an act of will and courage to concentrate on reconciliation. Carolyn thought it through carefully. She decided to be kinder to her sister, and she stopped trying to get her approval. That was a relief to them both. Then she realized that treating her sister like a mother, and being so needy, was part of her contribution to their difficulties, so she stopped doing that. Finally, she came to see that the conversations with her mother, in which they gossiped about her sister, were contributing to the problem. Perhaps her mother, an only child, had played a role in keeping her daughters at odds, ensuring that she would never be left out of the threesome.

Gradually, things got a little bit easier, and Carolyn's sister opened up. She confided some of her work troubles. Carolyn responded with understanding and compassion. Her sister was grateful for the support, and slowly the women found ways to be kind to each other. This was a new experience for them both.

Not everything went smoothly, mind you. There was a terrible crisis when Carolyn was about to give birth to her first child, a son. The sister desperately wanted to be in the delivery room when the baby came. Carolyn needed to be alone with her husband, and when she told her sister, all hell broke loose. Tears, screams, anger ensued. Carolyn understood that her sister took the delivery room decision to mean that she was being excluded from their lives. All those years of having her nose bruised by the slammed door gave Carolyn some empathy. So she told her sister, "It is going to be okay. We are going to get past this. We want you as a part of our life." She kept repeating, "It's going to be okay," and it by and large has been okay. "I mean, we made it," Carolyn tells me.

As we wind down our emotional conversation, I comment on Carolyn's determination to mend this relationship. "Now maybe she would say something different," she tells me. "Maybe she would say it was *her* determination." This comment tells me that the sisters are finding a way to connect, despite their past, their powerful differences, and their strong personalities. Carolyn was putting herself in her sister's shoes and giving her some of the credit.

This renaissance began in Carolyn's head. Her feelings followed, tentatively and sparingly. She wanted family, no matter what—and she was ready to ignore the grievances and tensions that had dominated their lives. I don't imagine that these women will ever laugh and cry and be silly together—it may not be in their natures. But they have the rest of their lives to deepen their connection.

Nothing worthwhile is easy, I have learned, and nothing difficult is accomplished to perfection. Those laws of human existence hold for relations between brothers and sisters as they do in other situations. My beloved tai chi teacher started each lesson by reminding me that while I might aim for 100 percent, the perfect score, it is wiser and more realistic to aim for 70 percent. I think of this as the 70 percent solution. It is a great deal better than nothing, and people who achieve that 70 percent have reason to be proud and satisfied. Joyce is struggling for that 70 percent. She may never get there. Her relationship with her brother has points of genuine closeness, moments of rage, and patches of disappointment. Their task will never be simple. But building is in their blood. It comes from a family tradition. So does fighting and drinking. They battle alcohol and seek refuge in renovating.

THE BUILDERS

Joyce and Archie grew up in the late fifties in a working-class neighborhood in Detroit. This brother and sister come from a family of first-generation craftspeople who arrived in this country in the early years of the twentieth century, building churches and factories, houses and schools, as well as robust families. They were stonemasons and woodworkers and bricklayers. They were old-fashioned and not given much to conversation, but they knew how to have a good time when they got together. Joyce recalls, "The relatives would come over and play pinochle in the kitchen, and there was also strudel that my grandmother would make, maybe a little schnapps, a little bit of beer, and a lot of coffee, and I would be underneath the table and I would sidle up next to my grandmother's legs and just lean up against her and listen to the joviality. They would slam their knuckles down and they would slam the table and there would be lots of laughing and it was a wonderful place to be." (This was great, except when there would be too much liquor and loud arguments would begin.)

Woodworking and building projects took the place of conversation in this house. Grandpa had a workshop in the basement where he made small things and taught the children. Their father built larger things—including a fabled hot-rod car for Joyce's older brother. It's no surprise that both kids grew up to work with their hands. Joyce is a sculptor, and Archie is a superb restorer and craftsman.

But Archie was not a great older brother. "He never really

wanted to be around me," Joyce says, "and he was always poking and prodding and if I made a comment, then I would get slapped and told to shut up. It wasn't fun." Joyce adored him but felt that she was growing up in his shadow. The bad stuff began when Archie and his friend—actually the son of their mother's friend—started hanging around Joyce. They eventually lured her into the basement and initiated sexual behavior with her. She hated it, but she couldn't stop them, and Archie never protected her. This series of events is much more common than we think, and like most sexually abused kids, Joyce never told anybody. She was far too ashamed of the whole episode, which made her feel filthy and evil. Soon the other part of their family heritage clicked in, and both the brother and the sister were drinking far too much. They didn't get along; Archie was obnoxious to Joyce, and she was furious. But as in all long wars, there would be periods of truce, and they always happened when the two of them collaborated on a project. Archie helped Joyce remodel her studio when she was starting out, and she tells me that they would go drinking in the morning on the way to the studio and hit the bars after they were done. While they were drinking and working together, the tensions abated.

But when Joyce started her long journey toward sobriety, their shared past could no longer be washed away in booze. Joyce began to pull away from her brother. The warfare broke out in earnest when Joyce, who had been sober for about seven years, refused to attend Archie's third wedding. When her parents objected, she told them about the sexual abuse. They were devastated but decided not to confront Archie that day. Some months later, her mother couldn't control herself and blurted out her disappointment and sorrow. A woman with "perfect" timing, she accused her son on the day of the christening of his first child. Archie went into a rage. He denied everything. When they met again, he confronted Joyce with a hammer in one hand and a wrench in the other. Joyce says, "He started yelling and screaming at me at the top of his lungs with these fists holding these tools in my face." Joyce tells me he screamed at her, "What the fuck are you saying? I never did anything like that. I never put my cock in your cunt, and to me, that would be sexual abuse." Archie's defense proved her point. Joyce thought, "That never did happen, but plenty of other stuff did." Archie threw his sister out of the house, and they did not speak for nine years.

As often happens, the period of total silence ended. Joyce began to feel some sympathy for her brother, and I think she began to forgive him, not only for the abuse of her childhood but also for his inability to get sober. The reconciliation happened during another renovation. Their mother was in her late seventies, and she lived alone in a two-family house. The upstairs would make a suitable apartment for Joyce, but it needed work. Joyce paid Archie for his time, and again they made a terrific team. "He can make wood sing," she says. Joyce, the artist, has an excellent eye, and she knows what she wants; and Archie, the carpenter, is also an artist. One day when they were working together, Archie got as close as he could to an apology. "So, it was just the two of us working in the apartment, and he said, 'I guess I was never really a good brother to you.'" They don't face each other when they talk, but the feelings are expressed. "One time when we were working on the apartment, he had constructed something and he did an amazing job. I put my hand on his shoulder, and I said, 'Archie, you are amazing, this is incredible what you did here, look at this.' I went through all the different points and I said, 'You are so talented,

I am really proud of you, this is great.' He looked at me like I had two heads and he said, 'Wow, nobody ever says that to me.' "

Here's Joyce's take on it: "A lot goes on when we are working. My family is all about making things prettier, making them better, keeping them clean, and maintaining them. I can't even express to you how huge this value system is. What I learned in my family was, wherever we go, it's better than when we got there. This is just what we do. This is just who we are." Side by side they are able to have a relationship they cannot have face to face. "Actually, I like my brother," she says. "He's got a great sense of humor. The way we approach projects is very similar; we have the same work ethic. We have a lot in common. We actually get along quite well, and we enjoy each other's company. I like working together on projects, and so does he."

Archie is nearing sixty now, and Joyce is in her middle fifties, and their mother's house is complete. Joyce needs to find another project. Meanwhile, her work of forgiving and making amends has enabled Joyce to see the tiny ways in which her brother is changing. He has reconnected with some people he hurt years ago, and when she extended the olive branch, he took it.

He's still a jerk a lot of the time, and he still drinks too much. His life is a mess, and he isn't helpful when their mother is ill. Still, these troubled siblings are no longer antagonists. They shrug at the behavior that annoys and disappoints them, but the building never seems to stop. It may slow down, but it picks up again. This is how Joyce puts it: "It's like a renovation. It's a relationship renovation."

———

I know a woman who always resented her older brother, while admiring and loving him, too. He was mean to her when they were kids, keeping her out of his room, giving her noogies when no one was looking, perpetrating Indian burns on her wrists, and calling her "my fat sister" when his teenaged friends came over. He was the family rebel, in continuous conflict with his parents. The conflicts were about his performance. The first son in a family of women, he was expected to excel at everything, and to follow the life course the parents had carefully mapped out. He did not want to meet all their expectations, and that led to trouble. As he became an adult, he would rage and rail at them, and they would cower. My friend watched on the sidelines, siding with her parents and resenting her brother. He got more attention, of course, because he did engage with these parents. She always felt that she was less important in the family, and she may not have been wrong.

This brother and sister were virtually estranged after he married and moved as far away from the family as physically possible and she stayed nearby to take care of the parents and raise her own family. Their relationship worsened when, many years later, they fought over their father's will. They didn't speak for a decade. Most people in this woman's circle didn't know that she even had a brother, which was fine with her. The close friends she confided in agreed that he was awful. She nursed her anger and pain. Nothing could quell her resentment.

Then one day, out of the blue a letter arrived. Recognizing the handwriting, this woman felt her stomach turn. She placed the envelope facedown in a drawer for a day or so and then summoned the courage to open it. The contents amazed her. He missed her, he wrote, and he loved her, and he wanted to have a sister again. His sentiments didn't quell her anxiety, and the very sight of the handwriting still made her nervous. Some months later, when she felt a little calmer, she replied in writing, and an intermittent correspondence began. A letter would arrive, and a few months later a reply would be sent. When she felt she could talk to him, they would speak occasionally by phone, but those conversations were résumé talks; they chronicled the progress of family members but contained no feeling. She found them exhausting because of their superficiality.

She understood that her brother wanted to build a new relationship with her, but she could not bear to do it. It took years until she was ready to confront him directly about their past. Eventually she screwed up her courage to ask the question that had plagued her since they were kids: "What did I do to make you hate me so much?" He didn't hate her, the brother replied, "I just didn't want that pretty and bright little girl in my life." She could understand that; it's how almost every older child feels when the new baby arrives. After this encounter, his wife wrote on her husband's behalf, "He may have been a rotten brother, but he is a fine man." That struck a chord, because the woman had come to like and respect her brother's wife. A year later, they met for dinner. She was anxious about seeing her brother again—he still scared her—but when she and her husband entered the restaurant, she saw a slight, elderly man whose face lit up when he spotted her. He didn't seem like the scary older brother anymore. At that meal, this woman decided she could risk visiting her brother and his wife in their home.

It was the first time in over fifty years that she stayed under his roof. They greeted her warmly—like a sister, in fact. The house was beautiful, and he was clearly loved and very happy. They shared the foods of their youth and they reminisced. She began to understand that their experiences were very different, growing up in the same house, four years apart. Finally, she could see him as the good man his wife adores, and he began to see her as the strong and vibrant woman she is. He drove her to the airport, and on the way, he talked about the things that troubled him most, and for the first time in her life, she shared some of her sorrows with him. Waiting in the security line at the airport, she picked up a message he had left on her phone. He was in tears, thanking her for confiding in him.

On the plane home, my friend felt elated. A rock the size of a boulder had been lifted from her chest. As they were landing, the pilot came on the intercom and said that the wind flaps on the plane were malfunctioning and they were preparing for an emergency landing. Looking out the window as the plane circled and circled, slowing down gradually, she saw the emergency fire vehicles gathered on the runway. My friend was scared, and then she thought, "If I die in this plane, at least I have a brother." The plane landed safely, or I wouldn't be able to tell you her story.

Today, they aren't anywhere near as close as some of the brothers and sisters I have described in this book. How could they be? They were disconnected for most of their lives. But now there is ease and a degree of warmth between them. When she tries to reconnect with all her negative feelings toward him—ones she carried for over half a century—she can't find them anymore. They have faded away. It happened with her, and that's not so unusual, that when she connected as an adult with this brother, and he did with her, some of the heat and pain went out of her heart. This woman spent most of her life suffering with her feelings about her brother. They became a burden as she got older. The letter she had received decades

before expressed her brother's wish for his sister; now she realizes what a remarkable gift that letter was.

A friend of mine tells me that the Hindu religion speaks of a
time when people achieve a certain age and may go into the
forest. They have accomplished their life goals of marriage, and
children, and work. Now they enter a time when new choices
are available. Entering the forest, we may decide to reconnect
with people we have lost, or to distance ourselves from others.
But our first question as we enter the forest is about who we are.
Are we carriers of grief and rage? There are parts of the forest
where we may leave those feelings. Is there longing in our
hearts for those who we have hurt, and who have hurt us? There
is a place in the forest where we may find them. As we wander,
we may become tired and lose hope, or the passions we brought
with us may abate. We may need to sit awhile and consider the
leaves as they move in the wind, and we may drink a bit from
the rushing stream. Finally, as we leave this place, we may, if we
are very lucky, find what we have been looking for: our better
selves, the part of us that can love and forgive, play and dance,
mourn and cry, and look up to the heavens with joy.

ACKNOWLEDGMENTS

First, I want to thank Stephen Bank and Michael Kahn, whose book *The Sibling Bond* I edited back in 1980. It was the first major account of the powerful emotional connections among brothers and sisters throughout life, and it formed much of the thinking about the subject (including mine). Without their book, this one would not have been possible. Working with Marcia Millman on her wonderful book *The Perfect Sister* also played an important role in my education about the role of siblings in adulthood.

I interviewed nearly one hundred people for this book, and to each of them I give my thanks. I had the honor of spending time with two memorable groups of siblings. One family welcomed me into their homes in the Midwest, and another joined me here in my apartment for a joyful and rollicking afternoon. Thank you.

I want to thank Bart and Yvonne Connors for giving me

shelter during the summers, and Starbucks for making it possible for me to meet and interview my subjects all over the city. Michael Sesling and his crew at the Transcription Agency provided accurate and speedy transcriptions of the interviews.

Thanks to Phyllis Grann, my brilliant editor, and her colleagues at Doubleday, especially Jackie Montalvo and Andrea Dunlop. Nicole Dewey and Rachel Simmons have been stalwart friends during the writing period, and my water aerobics friends known as Joy of Wet sustained me with their interest in this project. Michelle Press and Jane Chesnutt got me thinking about sisters on our first trip to Africa. Tina Weiner, Liz Darhansoff, Roberta Sorvino, and Naomi Meyer listened until their ears were full. Carol Tavris gave me words of encouragement when I most needed them. And Mary Pipher has been an unending source of wisdom and encouragement throughout the creative process. Thank you.

My family, of course, is my rock. Jonathan Dolger, my spouse (and agent), never wavered in his support of this project, and he read far too many drafts with patience and interest. My kids, David, Josh, Jen, and Cathie, give constant joy and encouragement, and they brought more this year. Ruby, a sibling for Benji, and Tobey, a little Brooklyn charmer. I cannot describe the pleasure of interrupting the hard work of writing to spend time with grandchildren. Thank you, little ones, for making me believe in the future.